How Deep are the Roots of
INDIAN CIVILIZATION ?
Archaeology Answers

How Deep are the Roots of INDIAN CIVILIZATION ? *Archaeology Answers*

B.B. LAL

Aryan Books International
New Delhi

How Deep are the Roots of
INDIAN CIVILIZATION ?
Archaeology Answers

ISBN: 978-81-7305-376-4 (HB)
978-81-7305-377-1 (PB)

Published in **2009** by:

Aryan Books International

Pooja Apartments, 4B, Ansari Road, New Delhi-110 002 (India)
Tel.: 23287589, 23255799; Fax: 91-11-23270385
E-mail: aryanbooks@gmail.com
www.aryanbooks.com

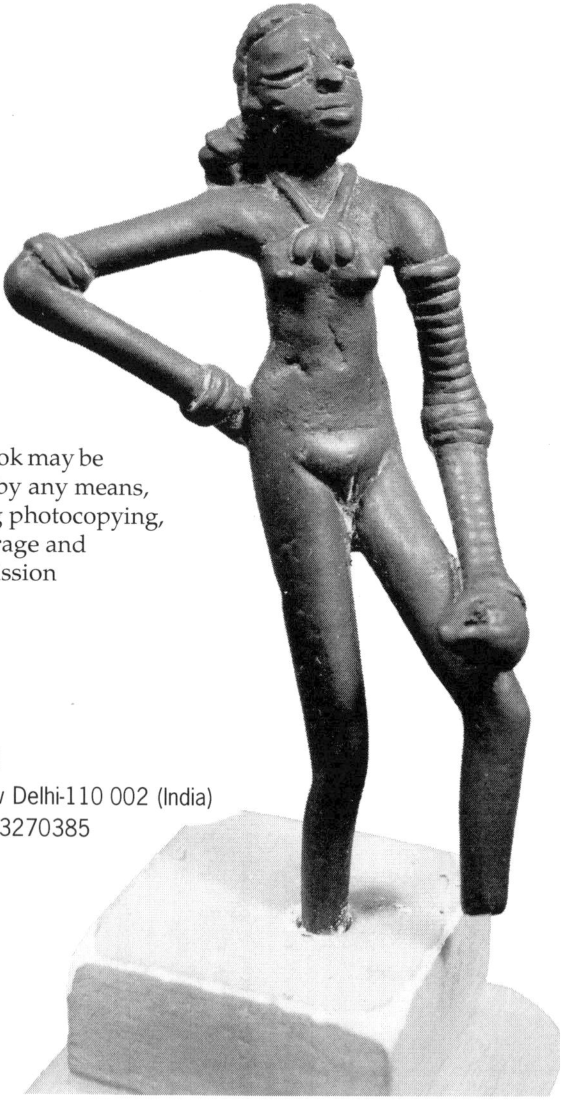

Printed in India

Dedicated
to
my most beloved student
Dr. S.P. Gupta
whose pursuit of knowledge
balanced judgement
unflinching devotion
self-sacrifice
and institute-building capacity
will ever remain enshrined
in the annals of Indian Archaeology

Preface

During the past ten years I have published four books, namely *The Earliest Civilization of South Asia* (1997); *India 1947-97: New Light on the Indus Civilization* (1998); *The Sarasvatī Flows On: The Continuity of Indian Culture* (2002); and *The Homeland of the Aryans: Evidence of Ṛigvedic Flora and Fauna and Archaeology* (2005), covering the various aspects of the most ancient civilization of India, which goes by the names of the Harappan or Indus or Indus-Sarasvatī Civilization. These also dealt, to some extent, with the evergreen controversy about the 'Aryan Invasion' of India as also the authorship of this great civilization.

As would be seen from the reviews that have appeared in various Indian and foreign journals, these books have been very well received in the scholarly world. While that no doubt gives me some satisfaction, I am greatly dissatisfied with another kind of feed-back that I have received. According to it (i) the presentation is too terse and scholarly for an average reader and (ii) the books are priced a little too high, somewhat beyond his reach. It is in response to this feed-back that the present book has been written. In it an attempt has been made to avoid scholarly jargons and to put the matter in such a way that the reader might feel that it is a kind of personal communication with him. This is particularly true of Chapter II which deals with the various cultural features of the Harappan Civilization that have survived the onslaughts of nearly 5000 years and can be discerned in one way or another in the life of the common people, particularly in the countryside (not so much in the metropolises which have become replicas of the West). However, in some of the other chapters the reader might find more details than he would have liked and references to publications beyond his need. But this has consciously been done, since, I am sure, some of the readers are likely to pursue the matter more deeply.

This book also contains a lot of new material, particularly that countering a strange twist given by certain scholars, namely that even if there was no 'Aryan Invasion', the Aryans must have still come from outside – from the Bactria-Margiana Archaeological Complex of Central Asia. Further, there is a chapter which opens up a new vista, namely that of 'Emigration' of a section of the Vedic people themselves to western Asia in the second millennium BCE.

With the ever-rising cost of production it is very difficult to maintain the high quality of paper and printing and at the same time keep the price down. Nevertheless, an attempt will be made to keep the price-tag as low as possible.

There is yet another departure in this book from the previous ones. While those were in large sizes, this one is particularly handy so that the reader can carry it about, and enjoy it (am I being too optimistic?) while on a plane or in a railway train or even in a moving car (of course, not while at the steering wheel).

All this has been done in order to ensure that the message of this book – which to my mind is more important than the messenger himself – reaches as widely as possible. At least let me hope that it does. I will await the next feed-back.

New Delhi
Independence Day
August 15, 2008

B.B. Lal

Contents

ACKNOWLEDGEMENTS

First and foremost, I would like to thank Air Marshal (Retd.) T.M. Asthana and his wife, Shrimati Kiran Asthana, our near relations, for kindly giving me their photograph with permission to publish it (Pl. I). I am also beholden to my daughter-in-law, Shrimati Sushama Lal, for the painting (Pl. XI) which illustrates how the well found in the Citadel at Dholavira was possibly used. My son, AVM (Retd.) Rajesh Lal, has gone through parts of the text and has made some useful suggestions. Thus, he too deserves my thanks. Likewise, my wife, Kusum, has also helped me in a number of ways in the preparation of the manuscript.

Outside the family, my thanks are due to Shri S.K. Sharma and Shri Vishnu Kant, my former colleagues in the Archaeological Survey of India. While the former has helped me by preparing some illustrations, in particular the map at Fig. 6.2, the latter has rendered useful assistance in proof-reading.

Finally, the buoyant publisher, Shri Vikas Arya, deserves my thanks for his ever-cooperating attitude.

List of Illustrations

FIGURES

PLATES

CHAPTER ONE

INTRODUCTORY

I am sure the reader must be wondering as to why it is at all necessary to tell him/her about the roots of Indian culture when he/she already knows that its source lies in the *Veda*s. But perhaps he/she is unaware of the fact that for the past two centuries or so sustained attempts have been made by many foreign and some Indian scholars not only to highly underestimate the date of the Vedas but also to misrepresent their contents. With such preconceived notions they are also reluctant even to consider that archaeologically the oldest civilization of India, known variously as the Harappan or Indus or Indus-Sarasvatī Civilization, could be the material counterpart of the Vedic texts. It is, therefore, proposed to present in this book a comprehensive picture of the Harappan Civilization, including the latest discoveries, and to discuss many issues connected therewith.

Of late, western scholars have coined a new phrase, 'the standard view', in order to impress upon the reader that all other views are 'non-standard' and, therefore, unacceptable. According to the 'standard view', the *Ṛigveda* is not earlier than 1200 BCE, though sometimes some authors do condescend to make it 1500 BCE. As would be discussed at an appropriate place in this book, the combined evidence of hydrology, geology, literature, archaeology and radiocarbon method of dating clearly demonstrates that **the *Ṛigveda* in no case can be later than 2000 BCE and may well have been very much earlier.**

These very scholars continue to chant, as if in a chorus, that the Ṛigvedic people were nomads – nothing but sheer nomads, without any iota of what is known as 'civilization'. As would be shown in subsequent pages, this view ensues primarily from a mis-interpretation of the Vedic texts, often combined with an undeclared highbrow attitude. This book will reproduce ample quotations from the *Ṛigveda* itself to show that the Ṛigvedic people were duly advanced, not only in metaphysical thoughts but also in matters that matter in the material world, such as construction of forts, producing surplus wealth, carrying on land- and sea-trade and even having a well established ruling hierarchy. Can such people be damned as nomads?

Although the 'Aryan Invasion' theory is now almost defunct, it has taken a new *avatāra* (incarnation) according to which, instead of an 'Invasion' there was an 'Immigration', from the Bactria-Margiana region of Central Asia. This too is a baseless proposition, as discussed in Chapter IV of the book.

There are two altogether new features that this book seeks to put forward. One, that archaeological evidence and Carbon-14 dates combine to show that the roots of the Harappan Civilization go back to at least the 5th millennium BCE and since there is a very good case for treating the Harappan Civilization and the Vedic texts as the two faces of the same coin, the Vedic people can very well lay claims to be all that old and hence indigenous to India (Chapter V). The other aspect that this book brings out for the first time is that a section of the Vedic people 'emigrated' to Iran and Western Asia some time in the 2nd millennium BCE. This is based on a combined evidence of archaeology and literature (Chapter VI).

Finally, contrary to Wheeler's claim that the Harappan Culture became extinct, most of its features – be these in the field of agriculture, cooking habits, sophisticated games played by children and adults, make-up by the ladies, religious practices and even the bed-time stories narrated by grandmothers to their grandchildren – have all defied the ravages of Time and are met with even today (Chapter II). In this context, one cannot but recall the words of the great Indian poet, Iqbal: *"kuchha bāta hai ki hastī miṭatī nahīn hamārī, sadiyon rahā hai dushmana daur-i-zamān hamārā."*

"Although world events have been inimical to us for centuries, there is **something** in our civilization which has withstood all these onslaughts." And that 'something', to the best of my understanding, lies in the spiritual foundation of Indian civilization, which allows a free inflow of fresh ideas, **without losing** the foundational ones.

CHAPTER TWO

From the Present back into the Past

(I) INTRODUCTORY

At the outset I must clarify one thing – in fact something very vital to our present discussion. It is this. When I talk of the Indian culture, I do not speak of urban India, of cities abounding in high-rise buildings and malls, with the Pizza-huts and McDonald's haunted by 20-25-year-young, jeans-and-top-clad girls (and, of course, boys). Urban India constitutes but a very tiny fraction of real India which indeed lives in villages. I am constrained to make this point since the cultural ethos that has been in existence in the country for over many millennia started undergoing vital changes since about the middle of the twentieth century – a change which is now increasing everyday, not by arithmetic but geometric proportions. I do not have any complaints about this change: this had to happen because of India's fast growing contacts with the western world, the inevitable 'globalization' and last but not least because of the small screen making silent yet steady inroads into every household.

I will now take up the various aspects of Indian culture, which are deeply rooted in antiquity – over 5,000 years old.

(II) MAKE-UP, ORNAMENTS AND TOILETRY

Please meet Air Marshal T.M. Asthana and his sweet wife Kiran (Pl. I). Surely, you will ask me 'Why'? In response, I will urge upon you kindly to have a second look at the photograph of the lady – a red streak along the medial partition-line of her hair. Isn't that obsessing? Yes, it is. But unlike most of the ladies at her level of social hierarchy, she unabashedly applies *sindūra* (vermilion) to her *māṅga* (the medial partition line of the hair) – a sign of being married, amongst Hindu women.

And now have a look at Pl. II. Do you know what it is? It is one of the many terracotta figurines of the kind found by a French excavator, Jean-Francois Jarrige, in his recent excavation at a site called Nausharo, in present-day Pakistan but forming a part of India before the 1947-Partition. On a closer look at the figurine you will realize there is something common between it and the photograph of Mrs. Asthana. The hair of the figurine is painted black so as to depict the colour, which is the same as in the case of Mrs. Asthana. But more noteworthy is the red paint in the medial partition of the hair, which similar to the *sindūra* (vermilion) applied by Mrs. Asthana. Of course, the lady of Nausharo shows off a series of gold necklaces (shown by yellow paint) coming down all the way from the neck to the breasts – something which Mrs. Asthana is missing. She seems to be content with two thin necklaces, one of pearls and the other of gold.

And do you know the context of these terracotta figurines? Perhaps not. These were found by Jarrige in levels that have been dated by the Carbon-14 method to circa 2800-2600 BCE, i.e. even before what is known as the Harappan Civilization (also called the Indus or Indus-Sarasvatī Civilization). Ponder over the high antiquity of the practice of applying *sindūra* to the *māṅga*. Isn't that strange? But let me assure you that this is as true as you and I: you the reader and I the writer.

* * * * *

Now that we have begun with a description of the make-up by the women folk, may I draw your attention to the damsel appearing on Pl. III? This is a bronze statuette from the Mature Harappan levels of Mohenjo-daro. Aware of her beauty, she poses with the head slightly drawn back, the neckless dangling between her breasts, the right hand on hip and the left on knee, as if in a dancing pose. However, mark specially the series of bangles bedecking her left upper arm. Would you believe that the practice of wearing a series of bangles on the arms is still prevalent (Pl. IV) amongst the rural women in parts of Haryana, Rajasthan and Gujarat – areas where the remains of the Harappan Culture have been found in abundance.

And here is yet another example of what rural women in north India have to offer. Pl. V shows, on the right, a newly wed lady whose face you cannot see, but the contour of the *dupaṭṭā* that hides her face simultaneously reveals that right underneath it, on the crest of the head, there sits something conical that is responsible for that kind of contour. Indeed, if she were to oblige us by removing the *dupaṭṭā* – which, of course, she wouldn't, we would see that a conical head-ornament has been tied to the tuft of hair in this region. The ornament is called *chauk* in Hindi. Having found such objects in his excavations at Harappa in Punjab, Pandit Madho Sarup Vats wrote in his Report (1940: 442): 'By Hindus in northern India *chauks* are regarded among the essential ornaments which every man, rich or poor, has to give at the wedding of his daughter-in-law. This ornament is worn chiefly on religious and important domestic ceremonies only.' Similar ornaments were also discovered at Mohenjo-daro, another well known site of the Harappan Civilization. And here we display one such example, in gold, from that site (Pl. VI).

Please also mark, once again, the series of bangles on the hands of the newly married lady on Pl. V. On the left in this picture may also be seen the mother-in-law, pondering over the likely future in store, yet exuding satisfaction on having got a daughter-in-law.

* * * * *

We shall continue with the make-up by the women folk and the gadgets used by them for the purpose. For example, while we find in the cities the use of plastic combs, with teeth on one side only, which have also found or are in the process of finding their way into the villages as well, the women in the villages were using until recently a gadget, called *kakai* in the Bundelkhand region of which I have a personal knowledge. (My mother used to comb her hair with this gadget.) Made of wood, it has teeth on two sides with a plain or decorated strip in the middle. It is of interest to note that

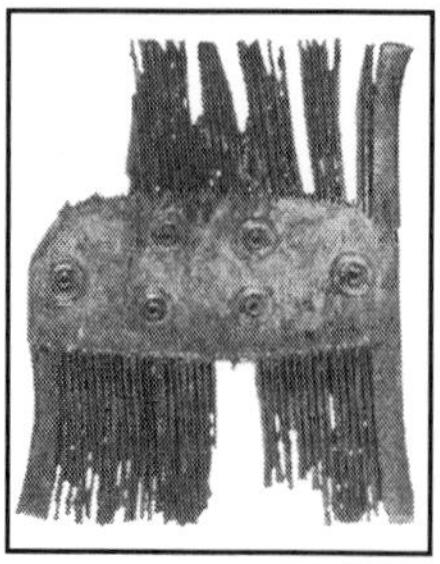

Fig. 2.1. Mohenjo-daro: Ivory comb with teeth on two opposite sides. Mature Harappan.

the same kind of gadget was used by the Harappans, some 4,500 years ago. The piece illustrated here comes from Mohenjo-daro (Fig. 2.1).

* * * * *

More than three decades ago when I was working at the Institute of Advanced Study, Shimla, I happened to visit the Lower Bazar there. Unlike the shops on the Mall at the upper level, this bazar displays all kinds of articles, some of which are specially meant for the rural people coming for shopping from the neighbouring villages. On a couple of the shops I found a three-in-one toiletry gadget, of copper, the like of which I had noted in the Report on the excavations at Harappa (referred to earlier). The two illustrations (Pls. VII and VIII) show respectively the gadget from Harappa and one from the market in Aligarh, the latter bought specially and photographed. Of the three pieces comprising the gadget, the one with pointed end is used for cleaning spaces between the teeth, that having a very small cup at the tip is meant for taking out wax from the ears, while the tweezer is used for plucking small-sized hair that sometimes grows on the inner side of the eyelids and thus becomes a source of irritation. Incidentally, I can well recall giving this treatment to my mother's eyes quite often since in her old age she began growing such hair underneath her eyelids.

(III) SOME CRAFTS

As a young boy of about twelve years, I often used to accompany my father to the vegetable market on Sunday mornings. Jhansi is a small town and the distances are not too long. I very much liked the sight of the vast array of vegetables brought straight from the neighbouring fields. Father too liked my going with him since he thought it to be a good exposure for me to the realities around. Sometimes he would include in his itinerary other odd jobs as well.

Roughly mid-way between our house and the vegetable market there was the house of a goldsmith, which was also his workshop. (His regular sales counter was elsewhere in the main market.) He was our family goldsmith and father told me that for the past quarter of a century he had been preparing ornaments for the family. I used to call him '*Sunār*

Chāchā' (meaning 'Goldsmith Uncle'). One Sunday morning father stepped into his house and told *Sunār Chāchā* that he (the father) wanted to buy a set of gold necklace, ear-rings and bangles for my elder sister who was to be married in the following winter. At the same time, he wanted to dispose of some gold ornaments which had been there in the family for well over fifty years and had gone out of fashion. Father had carried those ornaments in the worn out silken pouch wherein these had been kept all the time. He presented the ornaments to *Sunār Chāchā*. Seated on his small cotton mattress, *Sunār Chāchā* began to examine the ornaments. First, just visually and then using a gadget which seemed to me nothing but a small stone pebble. Yes, so it was. *Sunār* Chāchā picked up the ornaments one by one and rubbed them against the stone twice or thrice in each case. All this appeared to me quite funny. What was he up to?, I wondered. He showed to the father the various golden streaks that appeared on the stone as a result of the rubbing. He then added, this one shows that the gold used is pure, but this one is not all that pure. To my mind this was a very strange method of testing purity or otherwise of gold. Anyway, my father accepted *Sunār Chāchā*'s judgment and parted with the old ornaments for a mutually settled price. He then selected some new designs from the dusty catalogue and placed order for a set for the sister.

Believe me, I was taken by surprise when my colleague, Dr. R.S. Bisht, told me that he had found a similar stone in a house during the course of his recent excavations at the Harappan site of Banawali in Haryana. Even today, he added, it bears the golden streaks. (I am afraid I have not been able to get a photograph of it for you.)

* * * * *

Tourists to New Delhi, particularly those coming from abroad, are keen on buying typical Indian handicrafts. One may see these tourists jostling in the Handicrafts Emporium situated on the Janpath. But the prices there are on a somewhat higher side. Thus, those with a shoestring budget choose to do their shopping at the series of shops located on the western side of the same street, diagonally opposite the Emporium. Amongst the various objects that attract them are bronze/copper statuettes. Some of these are of a secular nature but mostly these represent various deities, such as Gaṇesh, Sarasvatī, Lakshmī, etc. Some of these are made by using a special technique called *cire perdue*. It is interesting to note that this very technique was used as far back as the Harappan times for producing some of the bronze/copper figures.

* * * * *

Today the area around Khambhāt (formerly known as Cambay) in Gujarat specializes in manufacturing beads of a variety of semi-precious stones. These are produced on a mass-scale and, besides being sold in the country itself, are exported to East Africa and neighbouring regions. The technique of producing these beads is briefly as follows.

The raw material, such as nodules of agate and carnelian, is imported from the Ratanpura mines near Rajpipla. These nodules are heated in pots placed in an earthen furnace. The heated nodules are broken into the required size and the desired shape is given by controlled flaking (Pl. IX). The beads are then polished by rotating them in a drum in which fine sand is also placed to achieve smoothness. Thereafter holes are bored by using drills to the ends of which are affixed roughly faceted bronze bits. Finally, the beads are heated once again so that these acquire a deeper colour.

Bead-making has been a profession of the Khambhātīs all the way back in time. For example, the Chinese traveller Hieun-Tsang (7th century CE) refers to the exporting of beads from India to Egypt on the one hand and to the far-eastern countries on the other. Likewise, a 1st-century CE evidence comes from the discovery of a large number of beads, along with the typical Red Polished Ware, from Nagara, which has been identified with Minnagar (Mahinagara) in the *Periplus of the Erythrean Sea*. However, it is the third millennium BCE evidence that is most exciting. Chanhu-daro in Sindh and Lothal in Gujarat have yielded ample data about the bead-making industry and we shall have a look at what the latter site has to offer. In the courtyard of a house in Block E at Lothal there was a platform in which two earthen jars had been embedded, one containing 582 beads of carnelian and the other 212 beads variously of carnelian, shell and steatite. A large number of cores, flakes, ground beads lay all over in the courtyard and some of the adjacent rooms. Nearby was also found a bronze drill-bit which apparently was used in boring holes through the beads. To the northeast of this area there was a kiln in which first the raw material and then the finished beads were baked.

The beads manufactured at Lothal and Chanhu-daro not only met the needs of domestic markets, but were also exported. These have been found at a large number of sites in contemporary Mesopotamia, Iran and Central Asia.

(IV) AGRICULTURE

I do not know how many of my readers have been to the countryside and seen for themselves the agricultural fields that surround the villages. Perhaps not many. Anyway, I am sure they must have at least noticed, while travelling by the railway train or even by road-transport, fields carrying a variety of crops during different parts of the year. In winter, anyone travelling in Rajasthan, Panjab, Haryana or western Uttar Pradesh is delighted to find fields greeting one with their yellow flowers swinging to and fro with gently blowing breeze. These are the mustard plants covering continuous hectares of land. If your mind is not already cluttered with thoughts, these vast fields can transport you to a land of fantasy. No words can create that mood; one has to have that experience!

In most of these mustard fields grams are also grown. The pattern is that while the mustard plants are grown in widely-distanced north-south furrows, the gram is sown in short-distanced east-west furrows (Fig. 2.2). This arrangement is not arbitrary. It seems to have emerged after a good deal of observation of the sun's movement. It is common knowledge that the axis of the earth is inclined and the earth rotates, on its own elliptical pathway, around the sun and completes the journey in a year. Thus, when the northern hemisphere of the earth is inclined towards the sun, it is summer there and when this hemisphere is away from the sun, it is winter. The result is that in winter, the sun, being farther away, casts longer shadows in the northern hemisphere – in our present context, in the areas comprising Rajasthan, Panjab, Haryana, etc.

The mustard plants, being much taller than the gram plants, cast much longer shadows than do the latter. Hence

Fig. 2.2. Kalibangan: Modern field with mustard plants in the widely distanced furrows and those of gram in the others.

in order to ensure that the long, northward shadows of the mustard plants do not fall on the gram plants and hamper the latter's growth, the former plants are grown in north-south furrows so that their shadows fall on their own fellow plants and not on the gram plants. Further, the furrows carrying the mustard plants are also widely distanced, thus leaving enough free space for the gram plants to receive sunlight.

It is interesting to note, though no doubt it is very surprising, that the same kind of alignment of the furrows existed in the agricultural field discovered during the course of excavations at Kalibangan in Hanumangarh District of Rajasthan (Fig. 2.3). The two sets of furrows cross each other at right angles. The intermediary distance between the north-south furrows is 1.9 metres, whereas that between the east-west furrows is only 30 cm. It may also be noted that while ploughing the fields, the ancient farmers of Kalibangan ploughed the narrow-distanced east-west furrows first and the wide-distanced furrow afterwards, as may be observed from the illustration (Fig. 2.3) which shows the wide-distanced furrows cutting the other ones. This is precisely what happens in the modern fields too (Fig. 2.4).

This Kalibangan field belongs to the Early Harappan times and is datable to circa 2800 BCE. When the Early

Fig. 2.3. Kalibangan: Criss-cross furrows of an Early Harappan agricultural field.

Harappans deserted the site because of an earthquake, around 2700 BCE, the field too naturally went out of commission. It got covered up by a deposit of sand and clay. Thus, when the Harappans returned to the site, after a gap of about a century or so, they were not aware of its location, with the result that some of their houses were built over a part of this field, as may be observed in the top left corner of Fig. 2.3.

Incidentally, one need not be surprised if one fine morning the Kalibangan farmer of the early third millennium BCE rises from his grave and insists on suing the modern farmer for the latter having copied his system of ploughing and cropping, without his prior permission!

The story does not end with the criss-cross system of ploughing the fields. Even the ploughshare with which the agricultural fields are ploughed nowadays has its ancient counterpart. The terracotta model of a ploughshare displayed here (Fig. 2.5) was found in the Harappan levels of Banawali in Haryana. (In the hot and humid climate of our country, it would be too much to expect a wooden example to have survived.) With its beam and sharpened 'shoe', the terracotta model from Banawali duly resembles the modern examples. May it be added that many more specimens have been found at Banawali itself and at other Harappan sites.

Fig. 2.4. Kalibangan: Modern system of ploughing, which also has a criss-cross pattern.

For raising crops a lot of water-supply is required. Though the rain does the basic job, it has to be supplemented with other means, such as canals, dams/tanks and draw-wells. While there is some evidence of canals dating back to the Harappan times, Dholavira shows that the local people dammed the nearby rivulets to ensure water-supply. They also dug up very large and deep tanks, but whether these were used for irrigating fields is not certain.

There is one more way of obtaining water-supply. It is from wells, using some special techniques. People living in cities and used to getting their water-supply from taps may not even know that there existed, until recently, certain devices to raise water from wells, particularly if the water-table was low. (For all one knows, in remote villages these may be in use even now.) In one of these devices, a large container made of animal-skin is used. Its two ends are tied to long ropes one of which passes over a pulley fixed on poles above the top of the well, while the other passes over the stone-sill placed at the rim of the well. Both these ropes are tied to the yoke which is placed on the necks of a pair of bullocks. These animals are made to walk up and down a ramp. Thus, when the animals walk up the ramp the leather container goes down into the well and on reaching the water-level gets filled up with water. When the animals perform

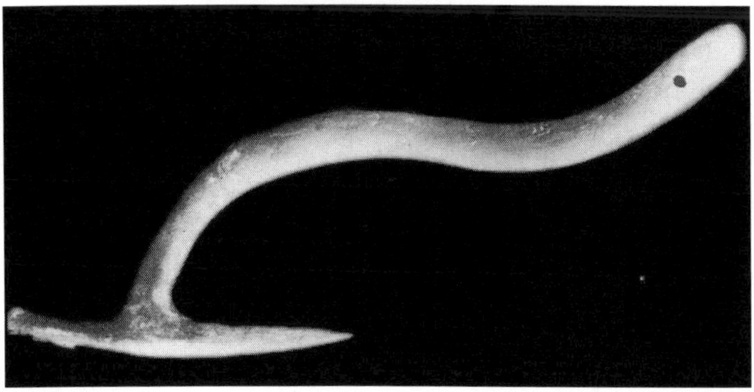

Fig. 2.5. Banawali: Terracotta model of a plough. Mature Harappan.

their downward journey, the bag is carried up and on reaching the rim of the well it unloads the water into a stone trough. From there it is carried by means of channels to wherever it is needed. The lower rope keeps on rubbing against the stone-slab of the trough and in course of time leaves deep marks on its edge.

The excavation at Dholavira has brought to light a well of the Harappan times, which tallies in all details with the kind of modern well we have just described. It has a trough at its rim-level (Pl. X). The trough consists of a flat slab at the bottom and three vertical slabs standing on its three sides (barring, understandably, the side from which the water-bag is brought up). There is a large hole in one of the side-slabs through which the water used to go out, falling into a channel which in turn carried it to two tanks in the neighbourhood. What, however, is most exciting is that the lower rope which used to rub against the well-side edge of the bottom slab still shows the abrasion-marks left by the constant rubbing of the rope (Pl. X; unfortunately, the abrasion-marks have not come out very clearly in the photograph). Thus, it is evident that this particular technique of drawing water from wells, discussed in detail in the previous paragraph, is as old as 4,500 years. (Pl. XI seeks to reconstruct what may have been the scenario in the case of Dholavira.)

(V) COOKING

'I am not all that hungry, but surely I must have *tandūrī* chicken and freshly baked *tandūrī roṭī*, for both of which your restaurant is said to be famous', told Abdul Rahim to the waiter, at the Moti Mahal in Daryaganj, Delhi. He had never visited that restaurant before. The waiter took hardly fifteen minutes and the food was on Abdul's table. A little later, just when Abdul was about to finish, the waiter appeared once again and asked, 'Sir, may I get you some more?'. Abdul was nearly full, but he could not resist the temptation and ordered another helping. Both the *tandūrī* chicken and *roṭī* were something out of the heavens. And the *tandūr* had done it all.

But would you believe that the *tandūr*, which is a special feature of the cooking paraphernalia of Panjab, northern Rajasthan, Haryana and Delhi, was already there in this very region more than 4,700 years ago? If you don't, have a look at Fig. 2.6, which illustrates four *tandūr*s met with in the Early Harappan levels at Kalibangan!

On return to his house, Abdul narrated all about the excellent meal that he had at Moti Mahal to his elderly cousin, who had come to Delhi a few days back to undergo medical treatment in respect his stomach ailments. 'But I am not interested in *tandūrī roṭī*s. These are too tough to digest, howsoever tasty these might be', retorted the cousin. He showed his preference for *chapātī*s (thin loaves of bread) and added that his mother prepares excellent *chapātī*s, not in a *tandūr* but on a *chūlhā*. The cousin lives in an interior village in western Uttar Pradesh, where the cooking-gas cylinder has not yet reached, and cooking has to be done on *chūlhā*s.

Fig. 2.6. Kalibangan: Clay *tandūr*s (cooking ovens). Early Harappan.

(Perhaps the city-wallahs would not know anything about them.) Made of clay, these *chūlhā*s are U-shaped and placed at the ground-level. Firewood is inserted from the open end of the U. *Chapātī*s, made of kneaded wheat flour, are first rolled over on a wooden/stone *chakalā/pāṭā* with the help of a wooden *belana,* and then transferred to a *tawā* which is placed over the *chūlhā*. When almost half-baked, the *chapātī* is brought down and placed against the edge of the *chūlhā,* where it is finally baked. If due timing is followed by the cook, usually the mother in this case, the result is a well-puffed and, of course, delicious *chapātī*.

It would interest anybody, as much as Abdul's cousin, that precisely the same kind of cooking arrangements also existed during the Harappan times. While digging, we came across in every house U-shaped *chūlhā*s with evidence of their inner sides having turned red because of the fire. We discovered terracotta *chakalā*s as well; these are circular on plan and provided with three short legs at the bottom. Strangely, in a few cases, these were even inscribed (Fig. 2.7). Was the owner so possessive of them? Or, did the potter – perhaps a specialist, want to leave his trade-mark on them. Since the inscriptions are pre-firing, it would appear that the latter was the case.

(VI) POTS AND PANS

"Do you want a single-fry or a double-fry?" Sushama asked her husband, as the latter was approaching the breakfast table. AVM Rajesh Lal was dressed up to go to his office within the next 10 minutes. The office car may turn up any moment. Replied Rajesh, "Anything would do. I am rather in a hurry this morning, since I have to have a final look at the papers before the scheduled meeting at 9:30 a.m." Sushama took out the frying pan and within no time prepared a single-fry egg and served it with a toast and a cup of coffee. Rajesh had his breakfast and dashed off. Rajesh is my eldest son and usually all four of us, namely my wife, Kusum, myself, Sushama and Rajesh have the breakfast together, but this particular morning we let Rajesh have his go first since he was in a hurry.

With the nuances of the Harappan Civilization having deeply entrenched themselves into my subconscious mind,

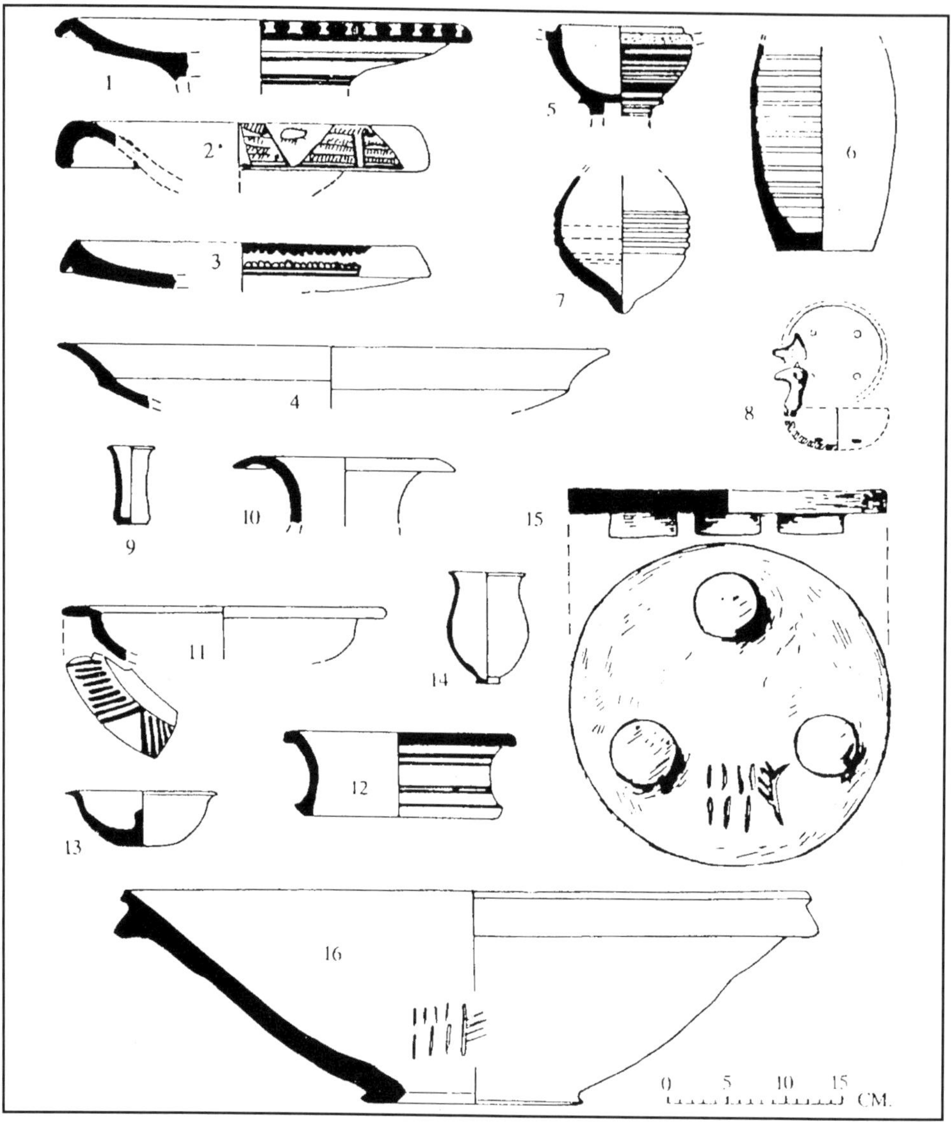

Fig. 2.7. Alamgirpur: Late Harappan pottery including a three-legged *chakalā* (No. 15), bearing an inscription on the underside.

I could not help pointing out to Sushama that the handled frying pan she had used for preparing the single-fry was exactly of the same kind as was used by the Harappan housewife some 4,500 years ago (Fig. 2.8: 4). In fact, even the *thālī*, *hāṇḍī* and *loṭā*, shown at nos. 1, 2 and 3 in the same illustration are no different from what are in use today. May

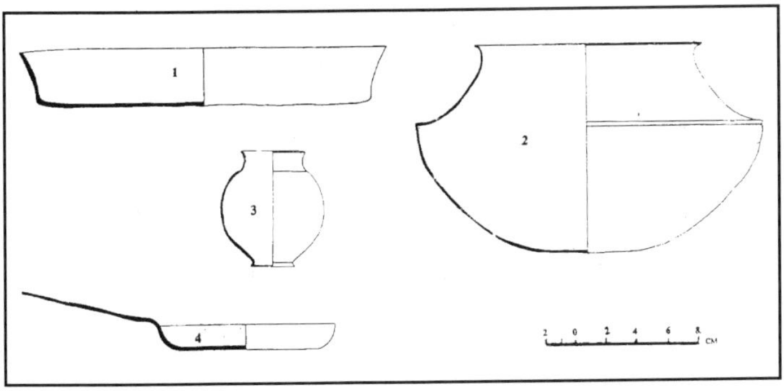

Fig. 2.8. Some Mature Harappan metal utensils.

it also be added that the *thālī* with raised sides is very popular with the labourers in eastern Uttar Pradesh and Bihar, who quickly make a mix of the *sattū* (powdered gram) with water, almost gulp it and rush on to the place where daily-wage labourers are recruited. Indeed, they cannot afford to be late, otherwise someone else may take their place.

Nowadays plastic bottles with a nipple-cap are used for feeding babies with milk. Often the nipple gets blocked and the baby struggles for the milk and cries. However, I remember that some seventy years ago my mother used to feed my youngest sister with milk by using a narrow-mouthed metal cup which had a long spout. The flow of the milk was uninterrupted and the sister enjoyed it all, sometimes even licking the nozzle of the spout. It would be of interest to note that the same type of feeding cup with an elongated spout was used during the Harappan times (Fig. 2.9). In the illustrated example one may as well note that at the junction of the cup and the spout there is the portrayal of a cow's face. Isn't there a touch of imagination!

(VII) PETS AND *PIÑJARĀS* (CAGES)

We live in a second-floor flat in Hauz Khas Enclave, New Delhi. It has a little terrace, facing a street within the colony. It is nice and cool out there and we often have our morning cup of tea on this terrace, watching and enjoying what goes on in the street below. Amongst other things, we watch the domestic servants taking out the dogs on a round. Most of the residents in this colony, supposed to be a posh one, have large-sized pet dogs, terriers, bull dogs and the like. (We don't have any. In fact, the very idea does not appeal to me

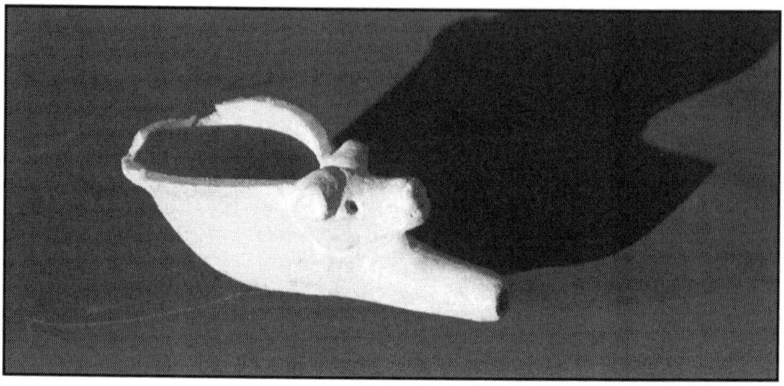

Fig. 2.9. Kalibangan: Terracotta feeding cup. Mature Harappan.

or my wife.) Anyway, these dogs wear around the neck a collar which, in turn, is attached to a leash. The servants hold the leash, keeping a control over the otherwise terrifying dogs.

Would you believe, readers, that keeping dogs as pets was also there in the third millennium BCE? If you don't, have a look at Fig. 2.10. Not being an expert, I cannot identify the breed of the dog, but can surely recognize the collar around the neck. Whether the Harappans also used a leash and took out their dogs on a morning round would, however, remain in the realm of guess.

As a child I was fond of petting birds, and my father willingly got me a pair of parrots. These were kept in a reed-cage, placed on a little platform located in a corner of the courtyard of our house in Jhansi. It was my daily duty to clean the cage and feed the parrots. Sometimes I would also open the window of the cage and let the birds feel free to go out and experience some freedom. The birds would often go out, only to get back soon into the cage. (Poor things, through long captivity, they had lost all sense of freedom.)

In my mid-twenties when I had a brush with the Harappan Civilization, on joining my *gurū*, Mortimer Wheeler (later knighted), at the excavations at Harappa itself, I started going through the report on the earlier excavations at the site by Pandit Madho Sarup Vats. It gave me immense delight to find in it a photograph of birds kept in a cage (Fig. 2.11). While one is already perched on the exterior of the cage, the other is trying to come out of the window, but they seem to be in no mood to fly away. A cage-psychology is after all a cage-psychology.

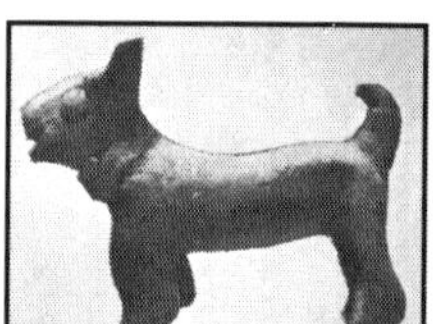

Fig. 2.10. Mohenjo-daro: Terracotta dog, wearing a collar. Mature Harappan.

(VIII) SOME GAMES THAT ADULTS AND CHILDREN PLAY

Chess is a game that requires patience, insight and, above all, an extra quantum of intelligence to anticipate the moves of the opponent – qualities, none of which I possess in the required measure. But there are others, particularly of the younger generation, who do have these in abundance and I cannot help recalling the moves of Viswanathan Anand who has defeated many distinguished players of the world including those from Russia who are acknowledged leaders in this game.

Fig. 2.11. Harappa: Terracotta cage, with birds. Mature Harappan.

While certainly Anand has every right to claim all the credit for his successes, little does he know that this game is in his genes: he has inherited it. His ancestors too, some 4,500 years ago, used to play this game. I am not joking. The evidence from two Harappa Culture sites, located far apart from each other, namely Lothal in Gujarat and Kalibangan in Rajasthan, have yielded evidence in this regard. At both these places have been found terracotta gamesmen that were used in this game. No gaming board, unfortunately, has survived, evidently because of the perishable nature of the material of which it was made. As we know, the chess gamesmen are distinguished, one type from another, by their shapes. While the Lothal specimens duly conform to this norm (Figs. 2.12 and 2.13), the Kalibangan specimens have an additional feature, namely many of these bear incised signs, in some cases even a short inscription indicating, for all one knows, their respective categories. So there we are!

* * * * *

Have you seen youngsters playing a game called 'Snake-and-ladder'? The die they use in this game is a cube bearing on its six faces 1-6 blind holes or circular marks (Fig. 2.14). When the die is thrown, the number that appears on the top surface is the one that matters. Based on this number, the player moves his/her piece. If, on doing so, the piece reaches the bottom of a ladder, the player has the right to move the piece up along the ladder. On the other hand, if the number takes the piece to the mouth of a snake, the piece must go all the way down to the tail of the snake. The game goes on until one of the players is able to send his/her piece to the top right-hand square of the gaming board.

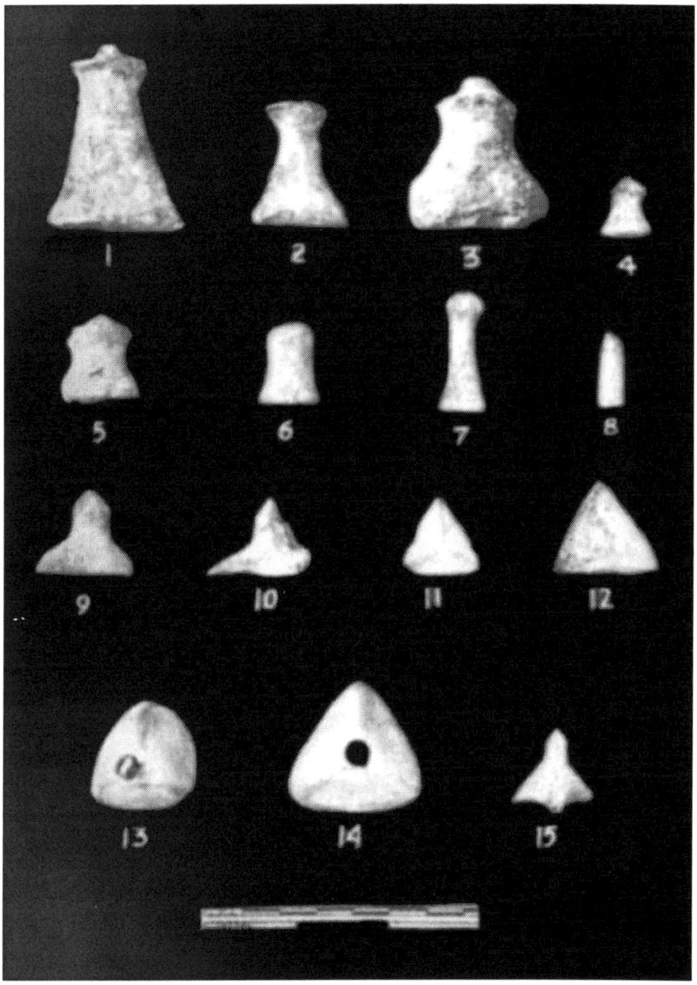

Fig. 2.12. Lothal: Terracotta gamesmen. Mature Harappan.

Though no Harappan gaming board has survived the ravages of time and climate, the dice, made of terracotta, have. Fig. 2.15 shows two such dice from Mohenjo-daro. It may, incidentally, be noted that in the case of these Mohenjo-daro specimens each blind hole was studded with a tiny disc bead. (These have fallen off in the case of the die on the right.)

(IX) WRITING AND WRITING MATERIAL

Perhaps it is not well known that all the Indian scripts – whether it be Gurmukhī of the north, Devanāgarī of the

Left: Fig. 2.13. Use of gamesmen in chess; reconstruction by S.R. Rao. The Lothal gamesmen are on the left and the modern ones on the right.

Right: Fig. 2.14. Modern example of cubical dice, with 1-6 blind holes on respective faces.

centre, Bangla of the east, Tamil of the south or Gujarati of the west – have evolved from the Brāhmī script which was used by the great emperor Ashok in the third century BCE for inscribing his goodwill message on pillars and rocks all over the country. Unfortunately, we are not lucky enough to have discovered so far any earlier inscriptions. And if there were any records on materials like birch, etc. these have all perished due to the hot and humid climate of our country.

Guesses have been hazarded about the origin of the Brāhmī script and two views seem to dominate the field. According one, the Brāhmī was borrowed from a Semitic script of western Asia, though there are not many takers of this view. The other view has it that it has been derived from the Harappan script of the third millennium BCE. And although there is evidence that the Harappan script did continue in one way or another – for example in the form of inscriptions on the megalithic pottery at Sanur in South India, which is datable to circa 8th-7th century BCE, there still remains an unbridged span of about five hundred years. We

Fig. 2.15. Mohenjo-daro: Cubical dice in terracotta, with 1-6 blind holes on respective faces. Mature Harappan.

Fig. 2.16. School children writing on wooden *takhtīs*.

can only hope that like the startling discovery of the Harappan Civilization itself in 1921, by the year 2021 we will have another startling discovery, bridging this narrow but vital gap.

But we certainly do have some very interesting material evidence about writing which links up the present with the past. Though the computer has entered the portals of primary schools, there are even today certain schools in the backwaters of the country where rectangular writing tablets of wood, called *takhtīs*, are used. Figure 2.16 shows one such school where the children are busy writing on *takhtīs*. These tablets have a small projection on the shorter side, which the children use a grip while writing. This projection has also a hole through which a cord forming a loop is passed, and it is with the help of this loop that the *takhtīs* are hung on a peg affixed to the wall after the job is done. Though, as I said, the use of such *takhtīs* is almost dying away, I can well recall myself having used as a child such a *takhtī*, learning how to write the Devanāgarī alphabets. I used to spend quite some time also on giving it a shine (called *ghotā* in my mother dialect, Bundelkhandī) with the broken bottom of a glass bottle.

There is very good archaeological evidence to show that the same kind of *takhtīs* were used by children in the third-second century BCE for learning how to write the Brāhmī script, as shown in the accompanying illustration (Fig. 2.17).

This is a terracotta plaque, recovered from a site in Haryana. The seated child is holding the *takhtī* by his left hand, while the right-hand forefinger points to one of the alphabets. Attention may also be drawn to the hole in the rectangular projection, partly covered by the left hand of the child. Through this hole, as stated earlier, was passed a loop of cord which helped in hanging the *takhtī*, when done with.

Fig. 2.17. Yamuna Nagar: A second century BCE terracotta plaque. It shows a child pointing out one of the Brāhmī alphabets written on a *Takhtī*.

But most surprising is the evidence that the same type of *takhtī* was also used as far back as the third millennium BCE. Though actual wooden specimens have not survived, obviously because of the harsh climatic conditions of the country, their exact models in terracotta have. Fig. 2.18 shows two such examples, both found during the excavations at Mohenjo-daro. These match in all details the ones used in the third-second century BCE and the modern ones, already illustrated. Not only are the Mohenjo-daro examples rectangular in shape, as their counterparts, but these also exhibit the small extension on the shorter side including the inevitable hole therein. Isn't fascinating – an unwritten history of writing tools from the present back by five thousand years?

(X) BEDTIME TALES TOO

It was 9 p.m. In a house in the vicinity of the Bhadrakali Temple in Ahmedabad, a 35-and-30-year young couple had retired to their bedroom, leaving the 5-year-young Lalo to sleep with her grandmother in the adjacent room. (The grandfather, unfortunately, had passed away a few years ago.)

'Why don't you sleep now, Lalo? It is too late in the night for you; you have to wake up early in the morning, get ready and catch you school bus', said the grandma to Lalo. 'No, *Dādī Mā* I am not yet sleepy. Anyway, I won't sleep until you tell me nice stories like the ones you have been telling on previous nights', replied the little one, hugging the grandmother more closely. 'Please, *Dādī Mā*, please'. *Dādī Mā* had to yield and she began:

Fig. 2.18. Mohenjo-daro: Writing tablets represented in terracotta. Mature Harappan.

"There was a deer who was very thirsty. He moved about in search of water and at one place saw a pitcher. Greatly delighted, he went close to it. But to his great dismay he found that the water-level in the pitcher was very low. He tried to insert his mouth into it so as to reach the water, but just couldn't. His long horns stood in the way and didn't let the mouth go down. After making several attempts, he realized that there was no way for him to get to the water. Greatly disappointed, he decided that he had better leave the place. Just then a crow flew in. He too was thirsty. He came close to pitcher. On finding that the water-level was low, he was upset for a while. But then a way out flashed across his mind. 'Why don't I collect with my beak some small pebbles and drop them into the pitcher? This will raise the level of the water and I will be able to drink it.' He did that and drank the water to his fill. The deer, who had not yet left the place, looked back at the crow, wondered at his wisdom, but still had to leave in disappointment now that hardly any water was left in the pitcher."

'Don't you see, Lalo, the crow proved to be more intelligent than the deer? What would you have done?' asked the *Dādī Mā*. '*Dādī Mā*, you feed me with so much of milk when I go out to the school in the morning that I won't have to look for water until I come back.' The *Dādī Mā* was greatly amused at the evasive reply of her grandchild. But Lalo didn't stop at that. She demanded another similar story to be told. She was getting fond of stories that showed the intelligence of the animal world. The *Dādī Mā* had to yield once again.

Began the *Dādī Mā*: "There was a fox. He started out in search of food. As he reached the nearby jungle, he saw two birds perched on the branches of a tree. Each bird was holding in her beak a fish that she had picked up from a nearby pond. 'Oh, how nice. Now is the opportunity for me to get my fill.' The fox thought of a trick, indeed unique. He told the birds that they were excellent singers, the like of which he had never seen before. Elated at this praise, the birds began to sing. As soon as they opened their mouth the fish dropped from their beaks. The cunning fox picked up the fish and ran away, leaving the poor birds brooding over their foolishness."

The above-mentioned grandmother-granddaughter episode took place in Ahmedabad in 2007 (CE). In 2007 BCE, hardly a hundred kilometres southeast of Ahmedabad, at Lothal, a potter was busy painting in black colour these very themes on his red-slipped pots. And here we present to the reader the drawings thereof. Fig. 2.19 shows a vase with a painted scene, the details of which are given in the panel below. Herein one may see, in a sylvan environment, the two main players, namely a deer and a crow, with a pitcher in between them. While the crow has just taken out his beak from the pitcher, the deer has turned his face backwards, with the eyes open in amazement. (Only one eye can be seen in the profile.) One of his front legs is outstretched, indicating that he is on the point of leaving. This is precisely the scene depicting the first story that the grandmother had narrated to dear Lalo, namely the story of 'The Thirsty Crow'.

Fig. 2.20 shows the story of 'The Cunning Fox'. While the upper right-hand part of the panel shows a pipal tree, it is the left-hand part that depicts the story. On the branches of an acacia tree are seated two birds, each holding a fish in its beak. The birds as well as the fish are cross-hatched. The portion beneath the tree on the lower right-hand side has unfortunately been defaced. But on the lower left-hand side one may see a small animal portrayed in solid colour. From

Left: Fig. 2.19. Lothal: A vase, the painting on which appears to narrate the story of 'The Thirsty Crow'. Mature Harappan.

Right: Fig. 2.20. Lothal: This painting, on another jar, seems to narrate the story of 'The Cunning Fox'. Mature Harappan.

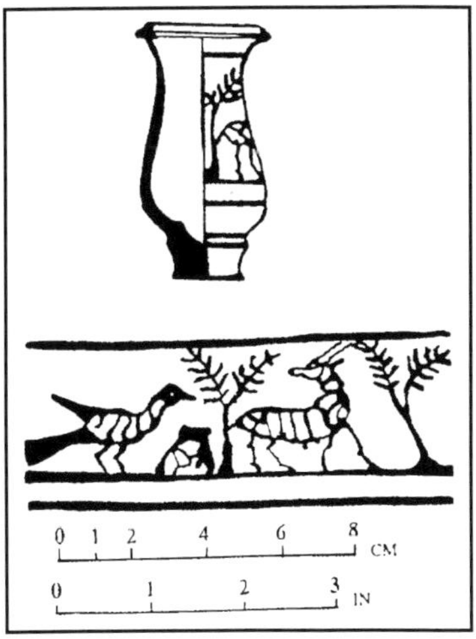

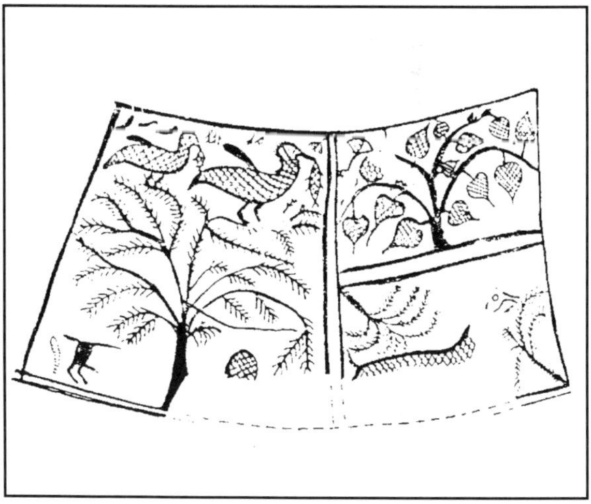

the way the tail has been depicted it appears that a fox was meant. Alongside it there lies an oblong hatched piece, maybe a part of the fish. (The artist could not obviously depict in this very panel the scene depicting the fall of the fish from the mouths of the birds and the fox running away with the same. For this, a supplementary panel was needed.)

(XI) YOGA

I am sure many of the readers must have watched Swāmī Ramdeva ji on the *Āsthā* Channel of the Indian Television, addressing thousands of people at *śivira*s (instructional camps) in different parts of the country – from Ahmedabad in the west to Guwahati in the east and from Shimla in the north to Bangalore in the south. He holds these camps to teach the aspirants the methods of *āsana*s and *prāṇāyāma*. This great Indian has revolutionized our thinking on these and has shown how to integrate the same in our everyday chores in order to make our life more healthy, free of mental stress and, in the sequel, enjoyable. He is a man who rose from the dust in Haryana, faced the problems of a poor family, struggled to set right his own health through *āsana*s and *prāṇāyāma* and has now risen to be a Messiah for others. Not only this, he has succeeded in establishing a very big institution named Patañjali Yoga Pīṭha, near Haradwar in Uttarakhand, to run his mission uninterruptedly. Hats off – perhaps he would not like this English expression – so *śata śata praṇāma* (a thousand obeisance) to this great soul.

The reader may not be knowing who this Patañjali is, after whom Swāmī Ramdeva ji has named his institution. He was a *maharśi* (a great sage) who lived around the second century BCE and wrote the renowned treatise called *Yoga-sūtra.* Full of aphorisms, it deals with *aṣṭāṅga yoga* i.e eight steps of the Yoga system as a whole. These are *yama, niyama, āsana, prāṇāyāma, pratyāhāra, dhāraṇā, dhyāna* and *samādhi.*

It may be surprising, yet it is true, that we have evidence of the third and seventh of these steps right in the Harappan times. (The other steps like *yama, niyama* etc. are of a theoretical nature and, therefore, it may be difficult to find tangible evidence for the same.) Of the third step, namely that of the *āsana*s, we have ample evidence in the Harappan Civilization. It is available in the form of terracotta figurines

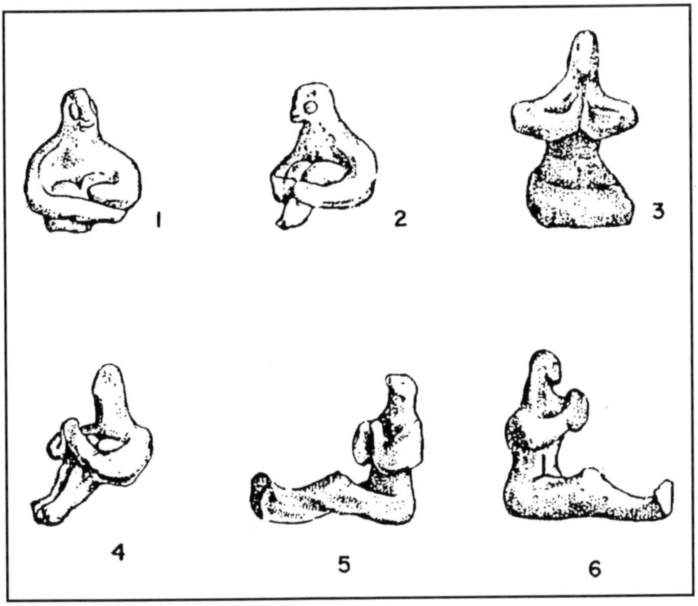

Fig. 2.21. Terracotta figurines in Yogic *āsanas*. 1-4, from Harappa; 5-6, from Mohenjo-daro.

engaged in performing the *āsanas* (Fig. 2.21). These specimens come from both Harappa and Mohenjo-daro.

In this context one may also draw attention to the famous limestone statuette of a priest from Mohenjo-daro (Pl. XII), which leaves no doubt that the figure is in a meditative mood. The eyes are introvert and eyelids half closed. This is precisely the mode of *dhyāna*, known to all those who practise it. While expounding the method of meditation, the *Bhagvadgītā* (Chapter 6, Verse 13) says '*samprekṣya nāsikāgram*' i.e. that the gaze should be fixed on *nāsikāgra*, which term has been interpreted by scholars to mean either the tip of the nose or its root. Elsewhere, the *Bhagvadgītā* uses the term '*bhruvor-madhye*', which means fixing the gaze in between the eyebrows. It is here that one of the *chakras*, namely the *ājñā-chakra*, is said to be located. It is at this *chakra* that the devotee has all his supersensuous experiences. In Western mystic literature this position is said to be the 'Centre of Christ Consciousness'. It is not unlikely that the priest may have entered even the last stage of yoga, namely that of *samādhi*, wherein all thoughts dissolve and what remains is pure consciousness accompanied by bliss. (Incidentally, one also notices the typical style of wearing the shawl by priests.

It emerges from underneath the right arm and then passes over the left shoulder.)

(XII) RELIGION AND RITUALS

Religion has two aspects. In one, it is philosophical or metaphysical, while in the other it is ritualistic. Man's religious quest probably generates out of his desire to know who he is, whence he comes and whereto he is destined to go. Further, when he finds that in spite of his efforts he does not succeed in getting the result he was aiming at, he begins to think that probably there is some unknown 'force' that interferes, marring his plans. He begins to search for this 'force' and thus comes into play the first aspect, namely the philosophical or metaphysical.

But not all of us are keen on this kind of inward search. Many think that 'that force' ought to be propitiated so that it becomes favourable. And thus comes into play the ritualistic aspect of religion. Erecting temples, churches, mosques, etc., making offerings, performing sacrifices and other acts of this nature come under this second category. This latter category leaves behind tangible remains which can be identified and studied even later, whereas the first category leaves no such concrete evidence except in the form of philosophical books, which may easily perish. The deeper we go into the past, the lesser the chances of our getting the books concerned, but the material remains, being non-perishable, are often met with during the course of excavations at ancient sites. Hence, here we take a look at which of the present-day rituals are traceable back in antiquity and how deep their roots are.

We have temples devoted to the deity called Śiva. In these temples there may either be an image of the deity or a symbolic representation in the form of a *liṅga*-cum-*yoni* (Pl. XIII). Would you believe that the worship of Śiva in the form of *Liṅga*-cum-*yoni* was prevalent as far back as the third millennium BCE, i.e. during the Harappan times? In the course of the excavations at Mohenjo-daro certain stone objects were found which were identified by Marshall as *Liṅga* and *Yoni* (Marshall 1931: Vol. I, Pl. XIV, 2 and 4; and 6 and 8 respectively). But, as is the case with all startling discoveries, some scholars doubted Marshall's identification. Recent excavations at Kalibangan in Rajasthan have, however, brought to light a composite representation of *liṅga*-cum-*yoni* in terracotta (Pl. XIV) which is similar to the modern example already illustrated. This leaves no room for doubt about Śiva worship being rooted in the third millennium BCE.

In this context it may also be well worth drawing attention to a seal from Mohenjo-daro (Pl. XV). On it is portrayed a figure seated in a yogic posture with animals surrounding him. Marshall suggested that the figure might represent Śiva in his aspect of Paśupati (Lord of Animals). The figure seems to have three faces, one in the front and one on each side. On this basis, Marshall went even to the extent of thinking that the figure might be the precursor of the concept of the *Trinity* (Marshall 1931: Vol. I, 52-55),wherein the three gods, Brahmā (the Creator),Viṣṇu (the Preserver) and Maheśa (the Destroyer) are represented in a single form.

* * * * *

From images we may pass on to rituals. The tourist itinerary in Kolkata often includes a visit to the famous Kali Temple. Amongst other things that the tourist might see over there is the offering of a goat to the deity. In the process, the poor animal is beheaded with a sharp weapon in front of the deity and it is thought this act will propitiate her. Kali is supposed to be the consort of Śiva. Though we have no representation of a consort of Śiva during the Harappan times, the concept of offering an animal to Śiva himself seems to have existed during that period. In this context we draw the reader's attention to the portrayal on a seal found recently at Harappa (Kenoyer 1998: Fig. 6.24b; here Pl. XVI). It shows, on the right, a deity. Because of its yogic posture and three-pronged head-gear, it resembles the figure of Śiva shown on Pl. XV, and may thus itself be that of Śiva. In the centre is a man and on the left, a buffalo. The man presses the head of the buffalo by putting his right foot on it and holds one of the horns of the animal with his left hand. In his upraised right hand there is a spear and with its sharp end he pierces the back of the animal. The scene seeks to depict the killing of the buffalo in the presence of Śiva, as a sacrificial act. It is learnt that in Himachal Pradesh the practice of sacrificing a buffalo before Śiva is still there. Further, it may well be that in the course of time there also evolved the practice of offering an animal to Śiva's consort as well. Hence the Kolkata scene.

That there did exist animal sacrifice during the Harappan times is further corroborated by engravings on a terracotta 'cake' found at Kalibangan. (In current archaeological literature such terracotta pieces have somehow come to be known as 'cakes', and hence the same term is retained here.) Though the 'cake' is broken, what was meant to be depicted by the engravings is fairly clear. On one side there is the portrayal of an animal. A noose goes around its neck and a man in front of it pulls it forward. On the other side of the 'cake' there is a figure with the typical head-gear, which characteristically resembles that of Śiva (Lal 2002, Fig. 4.57). Put together, the portrayals on the two sides of the 'cake' would indicate that the animal was being taken to be offered to the deity, namely Śiva.

* * * * *

In rural areas tree-worship is quite a common feature. On certain specific occasions, women-folk are seen gathering around a pipal (*Ficus religiosa* L.) or a *baragada* (*Ficus benghalensis* L.) tree and worshipping it. Not a very different picture of tree worship may be noted during the Harappan times. In the right-hand part of the upper register in the accompanying illustration (Pl. XVII) one sees a figure standing within an enclosure of pipal branches. On the basis of the trident-shaped headgear it may well be a deity and, if so, the manifestation of a 'pipal deity'. A human figure is seen kneeling in front of the deity and behind the human figure is an animal, maybe to be offered to the deity. But what is no less interesting is a group of seven human figures shown in the lower register. Evidently, these are worshippers. Isn't it an interesting case of tree-worship having its root in a 4,500-year-old cultural milieu?

* * * * *

I believe the reader is familiar with rituals in which *agni* (fire) plays a vital role, such as the *havana*. On special occasions, for example the inauguration of a new house (*griha-praveśa*), the *havana* is performed. A ritual fire is lighted in a *havana-kuṇḍa/vedi*, and the house-owner and his/her family sit around it and offer oblations into the fire. There are also much

Fig. 2.22. Kalibangan: A 'fire-altar' in a house in the Lower Town. Mature Harappan.

bigger *yajñas* in which hundreds of people participate and the *vedi* is much larger and of an elaborate type. How old are the rituals with which fire is associated? Archaeology gives the answer.

At Kalibangan and quite a few other Harappan sites, such as Banawali in Haryana and Lothal in Gujarat, certain fire-associated features have been discovered which have been called 'fire-altars'. (These, however, are not to be confused with the fire-altars of the Parsis.) Here we illustrate two examples of the 'fire-altars' met with at Kalibangan. One of these comes from a house in the general habitation area (KLB-2), and the other in what has been called the 'Citadel'(KLB-1). In the former example (Fig. 2.22) is seen a rectangular pit, about a metre in length, half-metre in width and 25-30 cm in depth. Its sides are plastered with clay which has turned red because of it association with fire. Within the pit one sees a vertical, clay stele. It is cylindrical in shape, has a diameter of 15 cm and a height of about 40 cm. The pit contains ash and charcoal, testifying to the use of fire. Around the stele were also placed terracotta 'cakes', circular-biconvex in shape. These appear to be symbolic offerings.

While the foregoing example, located inside an individual's house, relates to private worship, the example in the Citadel, located atop a mud-brick platform, seems to be associated with a kind of community service. In this case, there are as many as seven 'fire-altars' in a row (Fig. 2.23).

Fig. 2.23. Kalibangan: A row of seven 'fire-altars' discovered on a platform in the southern half of the Citadel. Mature Harappan.

(A subsequent drain, running across the series has almost obliterated two of the altars, but their existence can nevertheless be made out.) Though the altars are disturbed, stray remains of the stele and 'cakes' may still be identified within them; so also of ash and charcoal. The row of these altars is oriented north-south and behind them is a parallel-running wall. It would thus appear that the worshippers performing the ritual had to face the east.

There are two other features in this complex which call for attention. Right in front of the row of the altars there is a the lower half of a jar, buried in the ground. It is full of ash and charcoal, signifying that fire was kept ready in it to be used in the ritual. Within a few metres of the altars, to their northwest, there were a brick-lined well and a bathing platform, also made of bricks (not seen in the picture). This would suggest that taking a bath formed a part of the ritual. All these features – viz. taking a bath and facing the east while performing the ritual – remind us of the Hindu way of life.

* * * * *

I do not know how many of my readers have been to the *Kumbha Melā*, held every twelfth year at the confluence of the Gaṅgā and Yamunā at Allahabad in Uttar Pradesh. Perhaps some of them have. Spread over the Hindu month of *Māgha* (around January of the Georgian calender), it is perhaps the biggest religious event attracting millions of pilgrims. Besides ordinary devotees, the gathering includes several sects of mendicants (*sādhūs*) wearing special attires and holding distinctive emblems. Some of these *sādhūs* come out in groups on the backs of elephants. The elephants are highly decorated, their foreheads and trunks besmeared with a red paint (*kumkuma*). It is noteworthy that the recent excavations at Harappa have yielded terracotta figurines of elephant whose head and trunk bear evidence of red paint. Whether there did exist *sādhūs* during the Harappan times may remain a matter of debate, but the distinctive pot that they carry about, namely the *kamaṇḍalu,* has been found at Mohenjo-daro in the Mature Harappan levels (Fig. 2.24).

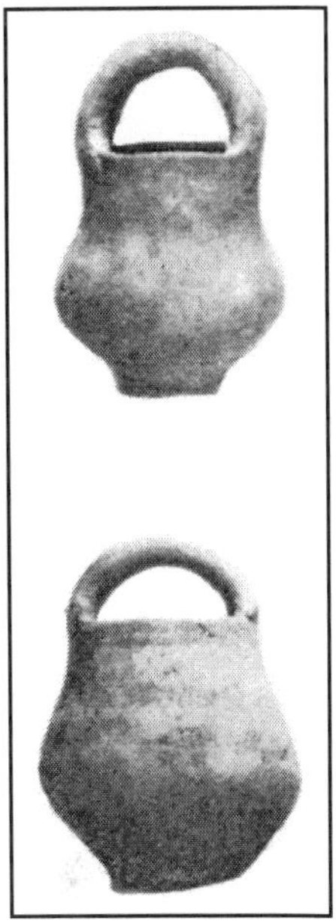

Fig. 2.24. Mohenjo-daro: Pottery *kamaṇḍalus*. Mature Harappan.

* * * * *

There are many symbols held sacred by the Hindus, amongst which the *svastika* occupies a prominent place. It is a sign of prosperity and good luck. The villagers often paint it on both the sides of the entrance to their houses (Pl. XVIII). Even the 'modern' city-wallahs, howsoever they may call themselves non-traditional, do succumb to the use of the *svastika*. I have myself seen many affluent residents of New Delhi painting the front and back glasses and even the bonnet of their newly purchased motor cars with the *svastika* symbol. Hidden somewhere in the subconscious, the tradition does surface up on certain occasions! Here, again, what is interesting to note is that the use the *svastika* symbol dates back to the Harappan times (Pl. XIX).

* * * * *

When two Hindus meet, they greet each other with folded hands, uttering the word '*namaste*'. This word consists of two parts, namely *namaḥ* + *te*, which respectively mean 'I bow' and 'to you'. Perhaps even many Hindus do not know that the term 'you' in the second component signifies 'God within you'. Thus, the obeisance is not to the physical body of the person addressed, but to God Himself. Be that as it may, on Pl. XX may be seen a former President of India, Shri K.R. Narayanan, being greeted with a *namaste* by the then Prime Minister, Shri Atal Bihari Bajpai, and his colleagues. It would be of great interest to my readers to learn that

Fig. 2.25. Śiśupālgarh: Air-view, showing the moat and fortification-wall around the 4th-3rd century BCE settlement.

greeting with a *namaste* was in vogue in our country as far back as the 3rd millennium BCE (Pl. XXI).

(XIII) TOWN-PLANNING AND ARCHITECTURE

Whenever a new city is laid out, it is always preceded by planning. Thus, when New Delhi was laid out in the first quarter of the last century, Lutyens conceived it in terms of circles and radii. Later, in the 1950s Chandigarh was planned by Corbusier on a grid pattern, the streets running north-south and east-west. Still earlier, in 1728, Jaipur too was laid

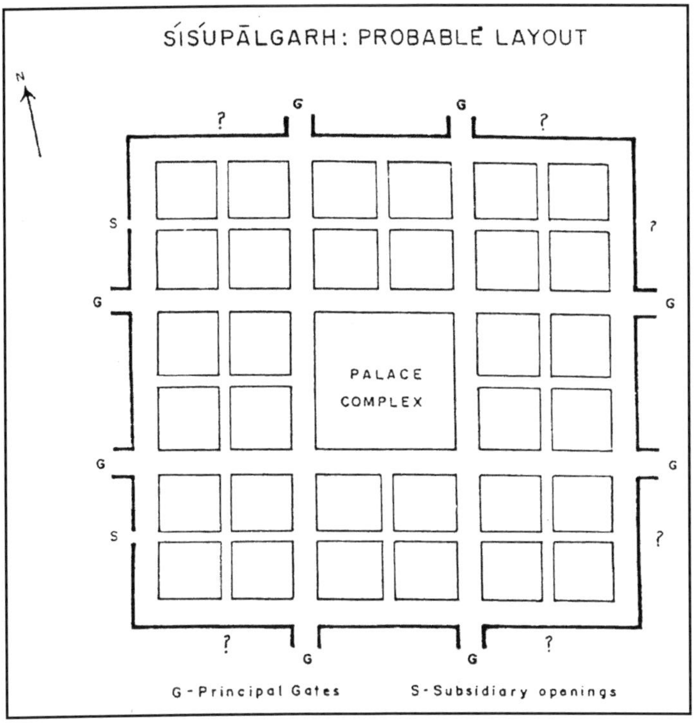

Fig. 2.26. Śiśupālgarh: Probable Layout.

out on a grid pattern. And when we get as far back as the 3rd century BCE, we have the example of Śiśupālgarh near Bhubaneshwar in Orissa, also following the grid pattern (Figs. 2.25 and 2.26). This grid pattern also seems to have been the craze with the Harappans; and we reproduce here a plan in which the Lower City at Kalibangan also followed the grid pattern, the streets running north-south and east-west (Fig. 2.27). It would thus appear that the grid pattern of town-planning has come down to us from the Harappan times. (It may, incidentally, be mentioned that civilizations, contemporary with the Harappan, in Egypt or Mesopotamia, had no concept of this kind of town-planning.)

* * * * *

And when it comes to the construction of walls, we find that what we now call the 'English Bond' was already there in the third millennium BCE. In this kind of bonding, the bricks in alternate courses are laid out (as you see them from the

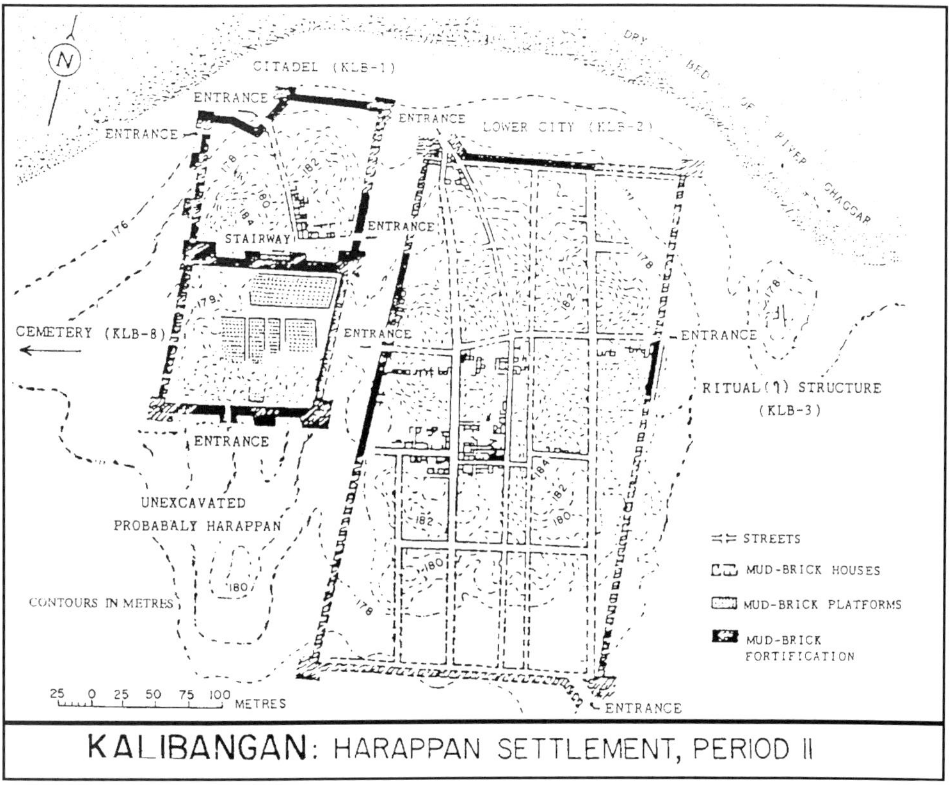

Fig. 2.27. Kalibangan: Harappan settlement, Period II.

front) respectively length-wise and breadth-wise. And as a proof of this kind of bonding having been used during the Harappan times we produce an example, once again from Kalibangan (Fig. 2.28).

* * * * *

But no less amazing is the continuity in the laying of floors in regions around Kalibangan. When we were excavating this site in the 1960s we came across successive floors in a house, which were made of clay but had underneath them a soling of fragments of terracotta nodules interspersed with large pieces of charcoal (Fig. 2.29). We really could not make out the significance of such a mix up in the soling. As chance would have it, some civil-construction engineers from the neighbouring town of Hanumangarh came to see the excavation. While taking them round the site we drew their

Fig. 2.28. Part of the fortification-wall around the Citadel, showing alternate courses of headers and stretchers (now called the English bond). Mature Harappan.

attention to these floors. They were surprised at this phenomenon and told us that this is exactly the kind of soling they too provide in houses which are located in a damp area. They further explained that the charcoal not only absorbs the dampness and thus prevents it from travelling upwards into the walls, but it also acts against termites. Shouldn't one give full marks to our forefathers some 4,500 years ago for this kind of ingenuity? (Incidentally, recently I happened to visit the resumed excavations at Harappa and was surprised to find that there too this very kind of terracotta-nodule-cum-charcoal soling was also provided in one of the houses.)

Fig. 2.29. Kalibangan: Successive floors of clay with soling of terracotta nodules and charcoal, in a house in the Lower Town. Mature Harappan.

(XIV) TRANSPORT, ON LAND AND WATER

India is a land of extremes. You have on the one hand the high-ups living in palatial buildings in cities, who always fly in the air whenever they have to travel, even owning their private planes, and, on the other, the tribals who reside in far off forests and for whom even a bullock cart is a luxury.

Fig. 2.30. Reconstruction of a bullock-cart, on the basis of terracotta samples of frames and wheels. Mature Harappan.

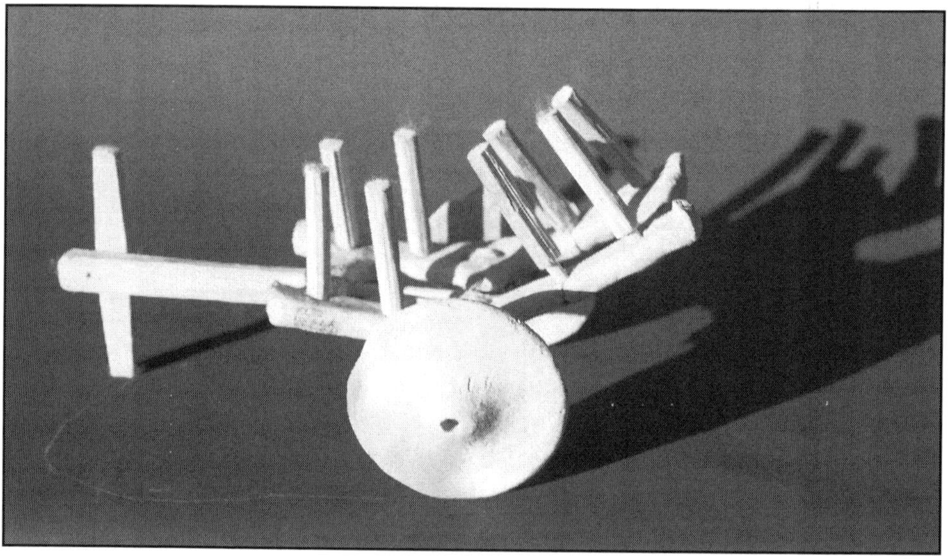

However, while the aeroplanes are things of only the past sixty years or so, the bullock cart is a vehicle since times immemorial. Excavations at almost all Harappan sites have yielded terracotta models of these carts (Fig. 2.30) from which one can easily reconstruct what the original wooden vehicles looked like. (It would indeed be too much to expect a wooden example to have survived our hot and humid climate.) But what is most exciting is the fact that not merely the shape but also the gauge (the distance between the two wheels of the vehicle) of the modern bullock carts has remained unchanged over the past five millennia! During the excavations carried out in 1946 at Harappa cart-ruts were found over the natural soil (Fig. 2.31). It was noted that the distance between each pair of ruts was 1.08 m, which, lo and behold, is exactly the same as in the case of the modern carts of the area.

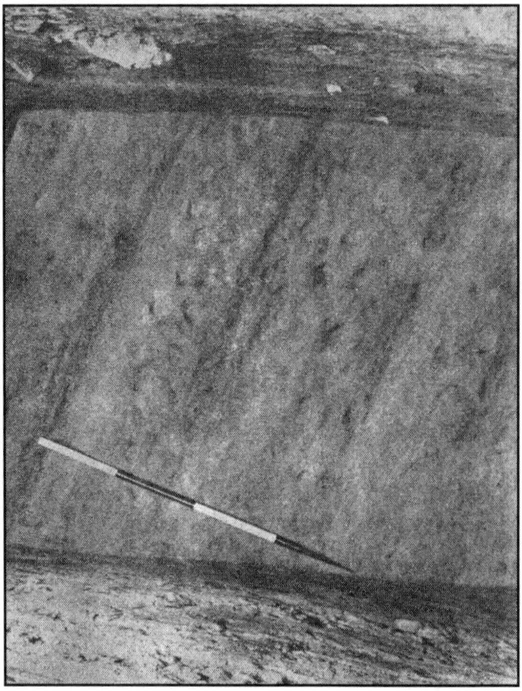

Fig. 2.31. Harappa: Cart-tracks, beneath Cemetery H.

* * * * *

Though we have large ships sailing across the high seas, we also have smaller barges sailing on the rivers or along the sea coasts. Fig. 2.32 shows one such boat parked on the bank of the Indus in Pakistan. It has a cabin in the centre and is

Fig. 2.32. A modern boat with a cabin, on the Indus in Pakistan.

Fig. 2.33. Mohenjo-daro: Impression of a seal, depicting a boat with a cabin. Mature Harappan.

characterized by an upturned prow. Similar boats were used by the Harappans some 4,500 years ago. Fig. 2.33 illustrates one such boat depicted on a seal from Mohenjo-daro. It too was provided with a cabin in the middle and had upturned prow and stern.

For use along the coast in western India, boats with sails are used. Lothal, a well known Harappan site in Gujarat, has yielded the remains of the earliest dockyard known to humanity. From here boats, loaded with cargo, used to ply along the Arabian coast all the way up to the Persian Gulf and Iraq with which area Gujarat had trade connections in the past. Lothal has yielded terracotta models of boats which have blind holes wherein the poles for holding the mast used to be fixed. Fishermen near the sea use nowadays long and narrow boats called catamarans. These are very convenient for fishing. Lothal, once again, has yielded terracotta examples which are similar to these catamarans.

* * * * *

By now, I am sure, the reader must have realized that most of our present-day cultural traits go back to the third millennium BCE. In the next chapter we shall try to present a somewhat detailed picture of the cultural milieu that obtained in our country during that millennium, and apprise the readers of the still deeper roots of that culture-complex – all the way back into the fifth millennium BCE.

Pl. I. Air Marshal T.M. Asthana and his sweet wife Kiran. Mark the streak of vermilion (*sindūra*) in the medial partition-line of the hair (*māṅga*) of the lady, which is a sign of her marital status.

Pl. II. Nausharo: Terracotta female figurine, painted. The yellow colour on the ornaments suggests that these were made of gold; the hair is black, while the red colour on the line of the partition of the hair indicates the use of vermilion. Period IB, 2800-2600 BCE.

Pl. III. Mohenjo-daro: The famous bronze statuette of a 'dancing girl', wearing spiralled bangles on the upper left arm. Mature Harappan.

Pl. V. A newly married lady, on the right, wearing a conical ornament on the head (covered by the *dupaṭṭā*). She also wears bangles all over her right arm.

Pl. IV. A lady wearing spiralled bangles.

Pl. VI. Mohenjo-daro: Gold cone. Mature Harappan.

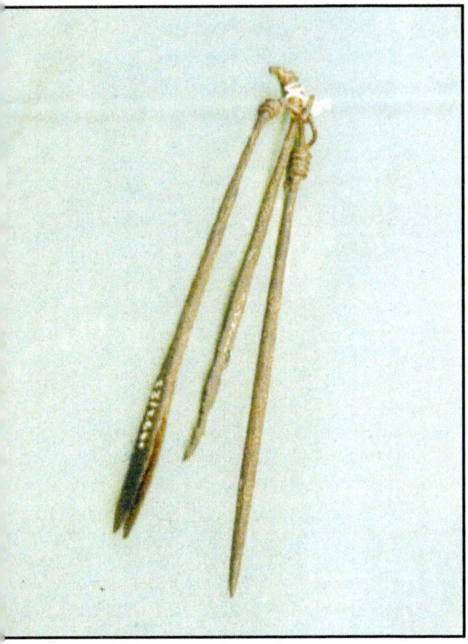

Pl. VII. Harappa: A three-in-one toiletry gadget, copper. Mature Harappan.

Pl. VIII. A modern three-in-one toiletry gadget, copper.

Pl. IX. A stage in the bead-making process, Gujarat.

Pl. X. Dholavira: A stone-lined well in the Castle. The flat slab of the trough (top left) bears abrasion-marks left by the ropes that constantly rubbed against it in the process of drawing water. Mature Harappan.

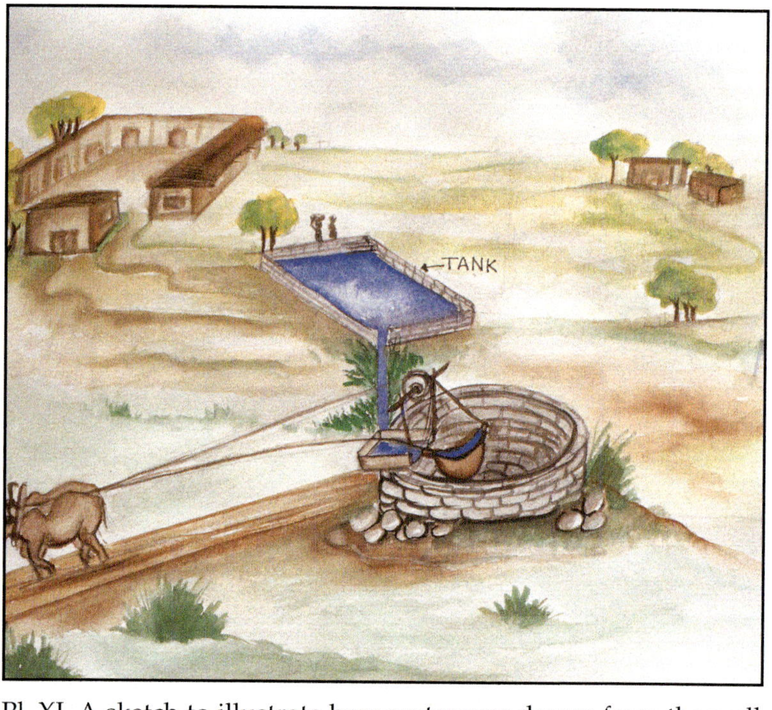

Pl. XI. A sketch to illustrate how water was drawn from the well (Pl. X). This very method was in use in northern India prior to the recent introduction of electrically operated tube-wells.

l. XII. Mohenjo-daro: Limestone statue of a priest'. The introvert eyes are indicative of 'hyāna mudrā (meditative pose). Mature Iarappan.

Pl. XIII. Śiva *liṅga*-cum-*yoni* in a modern temple. From the overhead pitcher water-drops keep on dripping on the *liṅga*.

l. XIV. Kalibangan: Terracotta *liṅga*-cum-*yoni*. Mature Harappan.

Pl. XV. Mohenjo-daro: Impression of a seal depicting a seated figure surrounded by animals, believed to be Śiva in his aspect of Paśupati (Lord of animals). Mature Harappan.

Pl. XVI. Harappa: Terracotta tablet, depicting the Śiva-like seated figure (right) and a person attempting to kill a buffalo, perhaps as a sacrifice. Mature Harappan.

Pl. XVII. Mohenjo-daro: Impression of a seal, showing in the upper register a deity within enclosure of pipal branches, a kneeling devotee and an animal perhaps brought in for sacrifice. In the lower register there are seven human figures marching in a row. Mature Harappan.

Pl. XIX. Mohenjo-daro: The svastika motif engraved on a seal. Mature Harappan.

Pl. XVIII. Entrance to a Hindu house, painted with the svastika symbol on both sides.

Pl. XXI. Harappa: A terracotta figure greeting with *namaste.* Mature Harappan.

Pl. XX. The President of India, Shri K.R. Narayanan (extreme left), being greeted with *namaste* by the then Prime Minister, Atal Bihari Bajpai (extreme right), and Shri L.K. Advani (centre) on the eve of the President's departure on a foreign tour.

Pl. XXIII. *Nyagrodha* (*Ficus benghalensis* L.).

Pl. XXIV. *Mayūra* (*Pavo cristatus*).

Pl. XXII. Kalibangan: Bronze bull. Mature Harappan.

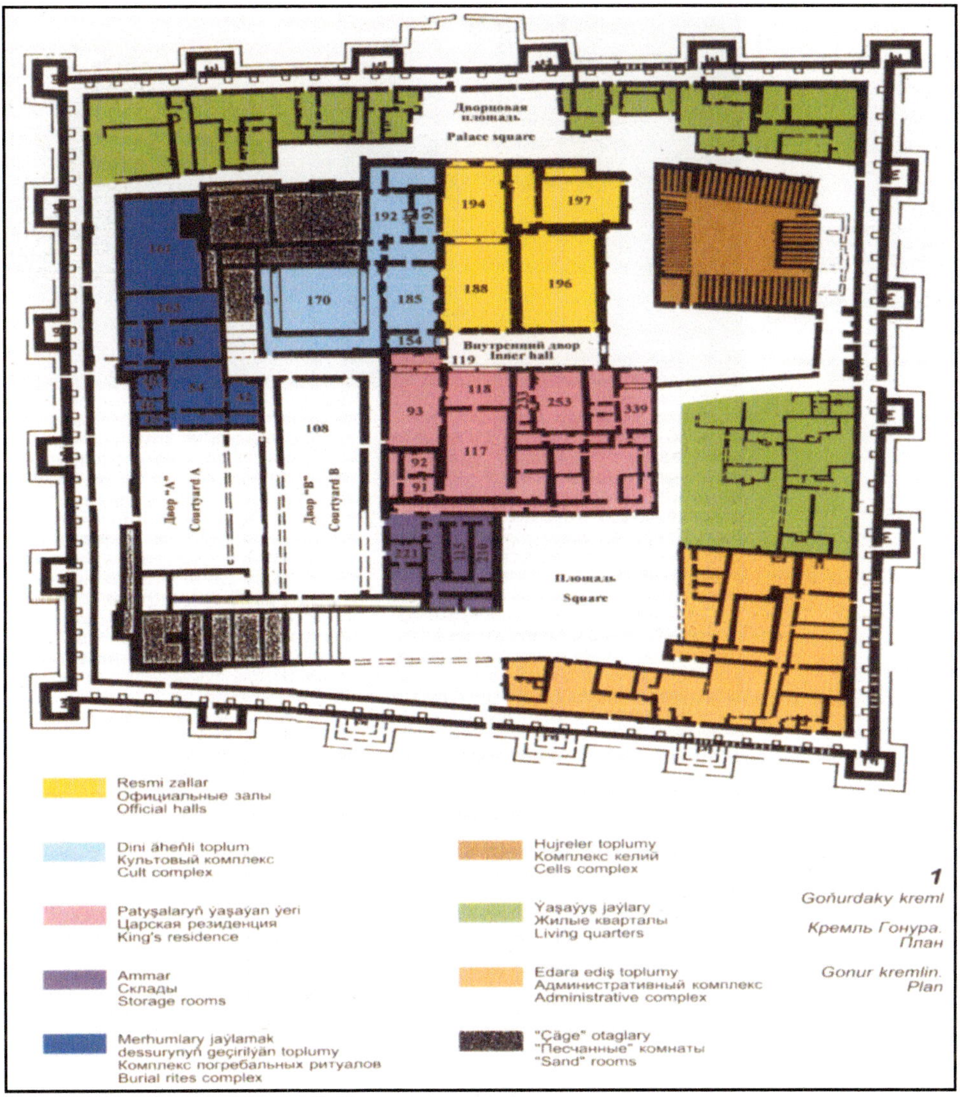

Pl. XXV. Gonur, Margiana: Plan of the 'Citadel'.

Pl. XXVI. Bactria: Bronze axes.

Pl. XXVII. Bactria: Silver ceremonial axe with parts covered with gold lamina.

Pl. XXVIII. Bactria: Composite stone figure.

Pl. XXIX. Bactria: Limestone goat, with horns, eyes and beard in lapis lazuli.

Pl. XXX. Bactria: Chlorite and gold leaf representation of a feline, with semi-precious stone inlay.

Pl. XXXI. Gonur, Margiana. Burial (?) of a horse.

Pl. XXXII. Rakhigarhi: Terracotta wheel. The painted lines radiating from the central hub and reaching the circumference clearly represent the spokes of the wheel. Mature Harappan.

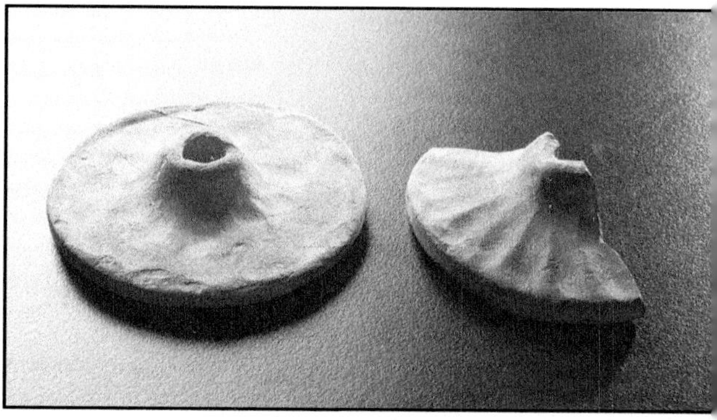

Pl. XXXIII. Banawali: Terracotta wheels showing the spokes in low relief. The specimen on the left is worn out but the spokes may still be seen. The specimen on the right, though broken, shows the spokes very clearly. Mature Harappan.

CHAPTER THREE

The Glory that was India – Five Thousand Years Ago

A. INTRODUCTORY

If you were to browse through the shelves of your nearest library and pick up the prestigious book on ancient Indian history, viz. *The Cambridge History of India,* Vol. I, you will find in it a remark by Sir John Marshall, the then Director General of the Archaeological Survey of India, that India had nothing to offer by way of ancient remains prior to the cyclopean wall of Rajgriha, ascribable to circa sixth century BCE. The great irony of it all is that while the book was being published (1922), one of Sir John's own officer in the Survey, Rai Bahadur Daya Ram Sahni, had in the previous year (1921) already unearthed at Harappa in the Montgomery (now called Sahiwal) District of Punjab archaeological remains which, in a single stroke, threw back the antiquity of civilization on the Indian subcontinent by well over two thousand years. In the following year, 1922, Sahni's feat was repeated by another officer of the Survey, R.D. Banerji, at Mohenjo-daro in Sindh. These initial discoveries were followed by large-scale excavations at the latter site by many Indian officers of the Survey, under the overall direction of Sir John. Subsequently, Mohenjo-daro was subjected to another spell of excavation by E.J.H. Mackay (1938). Harappa was excavated on a large-scale by M.S. Vats (1940).

With these excavations, it began to be universally recognized that India did have a civilization as old as those of Egypt and Mesopotamia. Further, the Indian civilization covered as much area as, in fact even more than, these two civilizations put together: from the westernmost site of the Harappan civilization, namely Sutkagen-dor, to the easternmost site, Alamgirpur, it is a whopping distance of 1600 kilometres, and from Manda in the north to Daimabad in the south the stretch is no less than 1400 kilometres (Fig. 3.1). But the extent is not that matters so much. What is more important is that even in certain qualitative aspects the Harappan Civilization excelled its counterparts. For example, neither of the aforesaid civilizations could boast of any kind of systematic town-planning, whereas the Indian civilization could. Over here the streets were oriented north-south and east-west, crossing one another at right angles. And to cap it all, running underneath the streets there were covered drains, with manholes at intervals, for the discharge of the sullage (for example at Mohenjo-daro). The use of kiln-fired bricks was another innovations at the Indian sites – something quite unknown to their western counterparts. While the famous statuette of the 'Priest' from Mohenjo-daro (Pl. XII) is a very good example of art in stone, and the ravishing 'Dancing Girl' (Pl. III) from the same site, of art in metal, nothing can beat the artistic grandeur and the technical excellence of the carved steatite seals. For who is there who would not be overwhelmed by the majesty of the zebu, with a full-of-vigour body and face, pronounced hump, large incurved horns and swinging dewlap (Fig. 3.17)?

Once the remains of this great civilization were identified, it was but natural to look for more sites. An important site added to the list was Chanhu-daro, excavated by E.J.H. Mackay (1943).

In 1944 R.E.M.Wheeler (later knighted) took over as the Director General of the Survey. His greatest contribution to Indian archaeology was to train a batch of young scholars in excavation techniques. One of the sites excavated by him was Harappa itself. Although an Indian officer posted at Harappa had already observed masses of mud bricks along the periphery of Mound AB at the site, it was left to Wheeler to dig this brick-work at a number of places and to identify it as a fortification-wall. The discovery was indeed epoch-

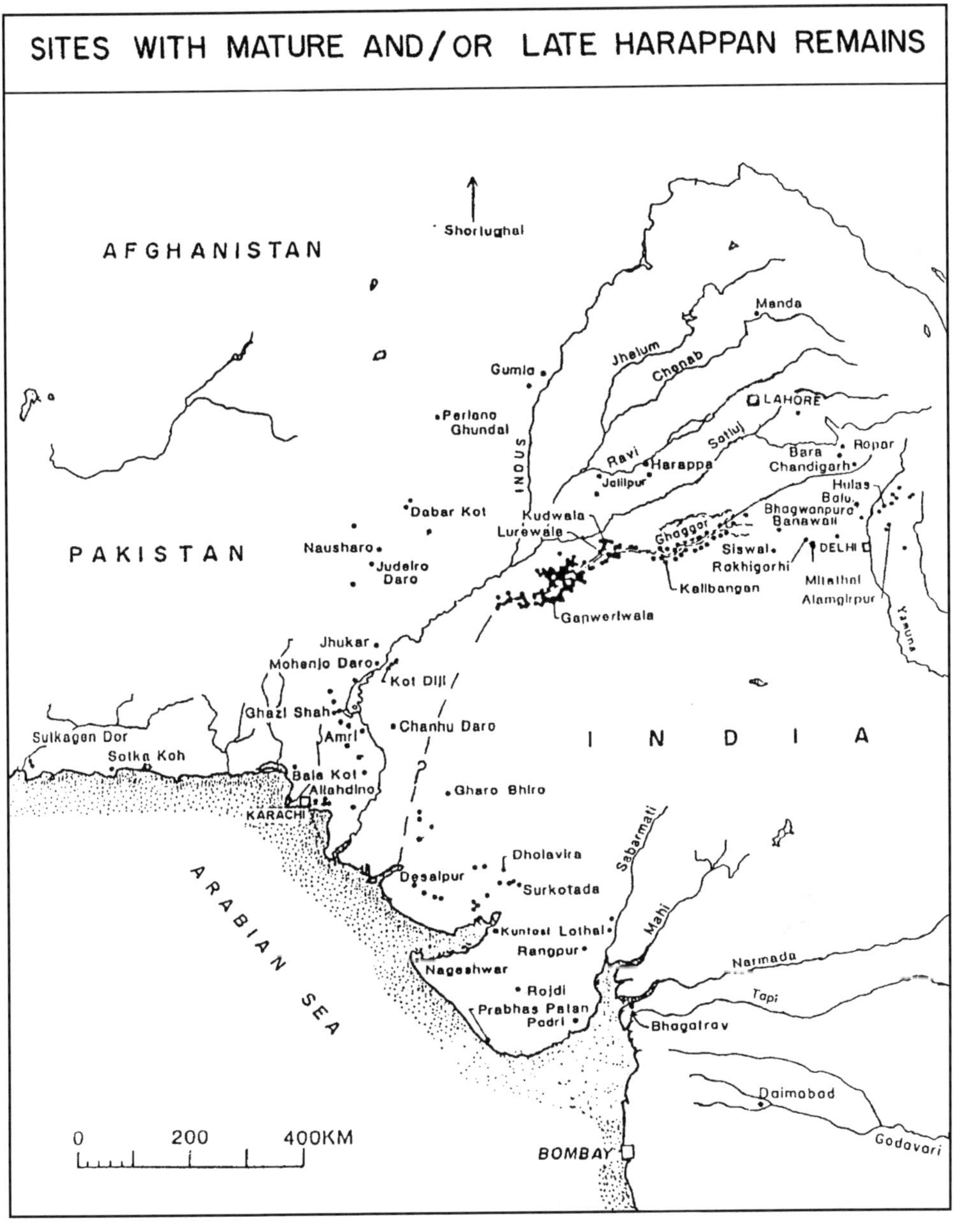

Fig. 3.1. Sites with Mature and/or Late Harappan Remains.

making, since right from 1921 to 1946 it was held that the Harappan settlements were unfortified. But the great master erred on the historical conclusions that he drew from this great discovery. He stated that Indra, who is mentioned as *puraṁdara* (destroyer of forts) in the *Ṛigveda* was responsible for the destruction of this fort. Extending his argument, he declared that it were the Aryans (whose cherished god Indra was) who invaded the Harappan sites, as a result of which this civilization became 'extinct' (Wheeler 1947). The fallacy of both these conclusions of Wheeler will be discussed later.

The mid-night of August 14-15, 1947 was as much dark for Indian archaeology as for the country itself. A large chunk of the country was carved into Pakistan and with it went over the two famous sites of Mohenjo-daro and Harappa, of course along with a host of others. Indeed, on the Indian side of the border there remained hardly any site worth the name of this grand civilization. The left-overs included a tiny little site, by name Kotla Nihang, in Panjab and a slightly bigger one, Rangpur, in Gujarat, whose Harappan association, however, was in doubt.

Indian archaeologists, however, did not lose courage but bravely took up the challenge and within a matter of a few decades brought to light a large number of Harappan sites within the bounds of divided India. In fact, today there are more sites, associated with the various stages of the Harappan Civilization, in India than in Pakistan. But the number alone is not what matters: it is the new light that the Indian sites have thrown on the overall character of this civilization. While we shall deal in detail with this aspect in subsequent pages, it may suffice to mention here in passing that the Harappan site of Lothal in Gujarat has given to the world the earliest dockyard, dating back to ca. 2300 BC (Rao 1979 and 1985). Dholavira, again in Gujarat, has thrown light on the unique town-planning unmatched at any other Harappan site. It had three units, all individually fortified yet integrated into a single complex. Besides, it has demonstrated how the Harappans dealt with the problem of water-supply. They harnessed the waters of seasonal nullahs and produced mighty reservoirs, cut into the bed-rock (Bisht 1991). The site of Kalibangan in Rajasthan has an Early Harappan occupation, besides, of course, the Mature Harappan. Associated with the former there was a ploughed agricultural field, which can easily claim the distinction of being the earliest (ca. 2800 BC) agricultural field ever discovered anywhere in the world through an archaeological excavation (Lal 1998). The Early Harappan occupation was destroyed by an earthquake around 2700 BC, which incidentally happens to be the earliest known earthquake in an archaeological context (Lal 1998).

With this little introduction, we may now go into certain vital aspects of this civilization.

B. SOME MAJOR SETTLEMENTS OF THE HARAPPAN CIVILIZATION

It has often been said that the Harappan Civilization was highly monotonous, both in space and through time. But recent excavations have completely belied this notion. And, as examples, we shall take up: three sites in the Sarasvatī valley, namely Kalibangan, Banawali and Rakhigarhi; Harappa in the Ravi valley; Mohenjo-daro in the lower Indus valley; Surkotada and Dholavira in Kachchha; and Lothal on the plains of Gujarat (Fig. 3.1). **It would be seen that each site was unique in its own way**.

(I) KALIBANGAN

It is located in Hanumangarh District of Rajasthan, on the left bank of the ancient Sarasvatī which is now dry and goes by the name of the Ghaggar. Within a perimeter of 1.5-2 km, the site comprises three mounds (Fig. 2.27), named from west to east, KLB-1 (Citadel), KLB-2 (Lower Town) and KLB-3 (a small, essentially ritualistic complex). The first settlement at Kalibangan, called the Early Harappan, seems to have come into being at the beginning of the third millennium BCE. Not much area has been excavated of the Early Harappan settlement. Nevertheless it was found that the streets were oriented east-west and north-south and the township was surrounded by a peripheral wall. The site, however, had to be abandoned because of an earthquake, around 2700 BCE (Fig. 3.2), but it was re-occupied after an interval of about a

Fig. 3.2. Kalibangan: Faulted walls and strata of the Early Harappan Period, resulting from an earthquake around 2700 BCE.

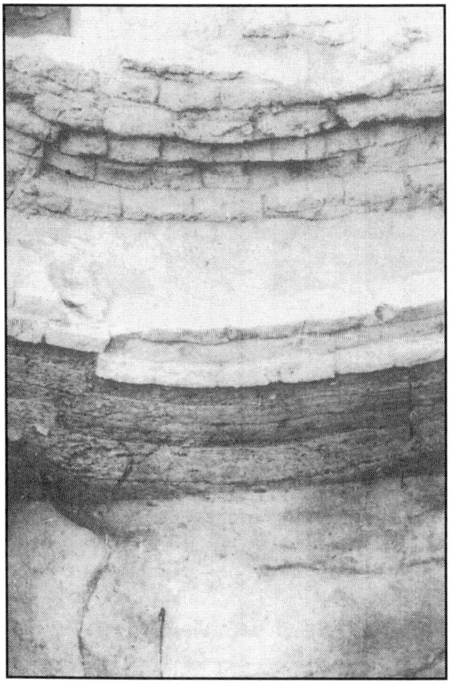

century or so by which time the people had reached the Mature Stage of development. What these Mature Harappans did was to build their 'Citadel' over the earlier mound so that they could get a higher position for it. The peripheral wall that went around it was in the form of a parallelogram, measuring 240 m from north to south and 120 m east-west. The Citadel was subdivided into two equal rhombs by a medial east-west wall (Fig. 2.27). Of these, the southern rhomb had a series of mud-brick platforms, with specialized structures on them, while the northern had residential houses with a street in between. This street went up to a gate on the river-front in the north. There was another gateway, on the east, connecting the Citadel with the Lower Town on the east.

Most of what once existed over the mud-brick platforms in the southern half of the Citadel has disappeared, but on at least two of these the overlying complexes could be identified. On one there was a brick-lined sacrificial pit containing bovine bones and antlers (3.19). In this context it may be recalled that an engraved terracotta 'cake' found at Kalibangan itself shows how the sacrificial animal may have been led to the altar. It bears on one side the animal with a noose around his neck, the rope being pulled by a man. On the other side, there is a figure which, because of the his headgear resembling that of *Śiva-Paśupati* of the famous Mohenjo-ḍaro seal, appears to be the deity to whom the animal was meant to be offered.

On the other platform there was a row of seven contiguous 'fire-altars', running north-south (Fig. 2.23). Behind the row there was a wall, which would imply that the worshippers had to face the east – something very significant in the Indian tradition. Though the fire-altars had largely been disturbed, one could still see in them the remains of a central clay stele, circular-biconvex terracotta 'cakes' (as an offering) and pieces of charcoal. Close by, on the west of this row of seven fire-altars, was found the lower half of a jar containing ash and charcoal, which suggests that fire was kept ready to be used for the ritual. A little away to the northwest there were a well and a bathing pavement, indicating that bathing formed a part of the ritual. (Here it is necessary to state the Kalibangan 'fire-altars' have little in common with those used by the Parsis.) There was a very wide entrance to this rhomb, through the southern peripheral wall. It was stepped, implying thereby that no vehicles could enter this part. Thus, all the worshippers were required to walk on the premises and not ride about.

In the residential buildings in the northern rhomb there lived the priests who supervised/conducted the rituals performed on the platforms in the southern. There was a long, mud-brick-paved passageway over which the priests may have walked in a procession, entering the southern half via a stepped entrance pierced through the medial wall.

The area to the south of the Citadel was unfortified. Herein only limited, exploratory digging was done. However, it was noted that the houses were small. In one locale a lot of pottery-waste was also met with. It is likely that this area was occupied by poorer people, including perhaps potters, who may have served the 'higher ups', residing in the northern part of Citadel and the Lower Town.

The Lower Town lay some 40 m to the east of the Citadel. This too was fortified, forming a parallelogram on plan (Fig. 2.27). Since the eastern and western walls were duly traceable, the width of the Lower Town was found to be 240 m. While the northern wall was clearly identified, the southern one had largely been eroded. However, it would appear that the north-south extent may have been in the neighbourhood of 360 m. Within the Lower Town, five north-south and four east-west streets were identified. It is interesting to note that the lanes/streets followed a set ratio. Thus, while the narrowest lane was 1.8 m in width, the streets measured 3.6 m, 5.4 m and 7.2 m respectively, making a ratio of 1:2:3:4. And what is most remarkable is that at no point of time during the six-seven hundred years of occupation of the site, did the Kalibanganites encroach on the streets (Fig. 3.3). Does this not speak volumes for their disciplined behaviour? The only structures that could be seen projecting into the streets were small mud-brick platforms adjacent to the entrance, which were a planned part of the layout.

An average house usually comprised a courtyard, on three sides of which there were living rooms, while through the fourth was the entrance, wide enough to let in even a bullock-cart. In the courtyard there were long troughs wherein fodder and water were kept for the cattle. In some of the houses the courtyard had a well. The rooms were

Fig. 3.3. Kalibangan: A Street in the Lower Town. Mature Harappan.

usually paved with mud-bricks, but sometimes with kiln-fired tiles bearing the design of intersecting circles. In another case, the floor consisted of a soling of broken hard-fired nodules interspersed with charcoal, over which clay was laid out (Fig. 2.29). As already stated earlier, this particular kind of flooring is laid out even today in the neighbouring villages, in order to prevent the sub-soil moisture from travelling up along the walls, as well as to act against termites.

Of further interest is the fact that one of these rooms appears to have been reserved for worship. In it 'fire-altars' have been noted in successive strata. An average altar consisted of a round-ended rectangular pit measuring about 1 x .5 m on plan and about 25 cm in depth (Fig. 2.22). The sides, plastered with mud, and the floor had turned red because of the fire which was kindled inside and has left behind ash and charcoal. In the central part there stood a cylindrical stele of clay, about 10-15 cm in diameter and 30-40 cm in height. Around it had been placed circular-biconvex terracotta 'cakes', perhaps as offerings.

The easternmost mound, the smallest of the three, revealed only fire-altars. Perhaps it was exclusively used for ritualistic purposes.

The area to the west of the Citadel was used as a cemetery. In it three different kinds of graves were discovered, to which we shall refer later in detail while discussing the burial practices of the Mature Harappans.

(II) BANAWALI

Proceeding 120 km northeast of Kalibangan, along the now-dry Sarasvatī, one reaches Banawali, in Hissar District, Haryana. The main mound covers an area approximately

400 x 400 m, and contains about 8 m of occupational deposits. Within it, three cultural periods, numbered I, II and III from bottom upwards, have been identified. These represent respectively the Early, Mature and post-Mature Harappan stages. While there was a continuity of occupation from Periods I to II, period III came up after a break (Bisht 1994).

The Mature Harappan settlement at Banawali presented quite a different scenario from that of Kalibangan. Thus, while at Kalibangan the Citadel formed an exclusively separate unit, in Banawali this was not the case. Here the Citadel lay within the overall area occupied by the Lower Town, the southern wall being common between the two (Fig. 3.4). For the rest, the Citadel had its own perimeter wall, and formed a rough semi-ellipse on plan. Excavation revealed the existence of houses and north-south streets within the Citadel. However, because of the limited dig it could not be ascertained if the Citadel contained platforms too, as it did at Kalibangan. There was a small gateway on the eastern side, and a ramp paved with kiln-fired bricks on the north, connecting the Citadel with the Lower Town.

A fortification wall surrounded the Lower Town as well. At one place on its east a moat was also identified (Fig. 3.5). While an identification of the moat on the other sides remains a desideratum, it is interesting to note the presence of this new feature in the Harappan system. The layout of the Lower Town was not on the grid-pattern, as elsewhere. On the other hand, fronting an entrance through the eastern wall there was a piazza from where the streets forked out in various direction, not necessarily cardinal. Some of the houses in the Lower Town were pretty large and their contents suggested that they may have belonged to well-to-do people. In one case, many weights and seals were found in it and its toilet 'was provided with a wash basin placed on a high place in a corner near the drain which carried off the waste water into a sullage jar placed outside on the street.' In another house, besides weights, there occurred a large number of beads of lapis lazuli, carnelian and gold.

(III) Rakhigarhi

In District Hissar, Haryana, there is yet another important Harappan site, called Rakhigarhi. It is located on the right

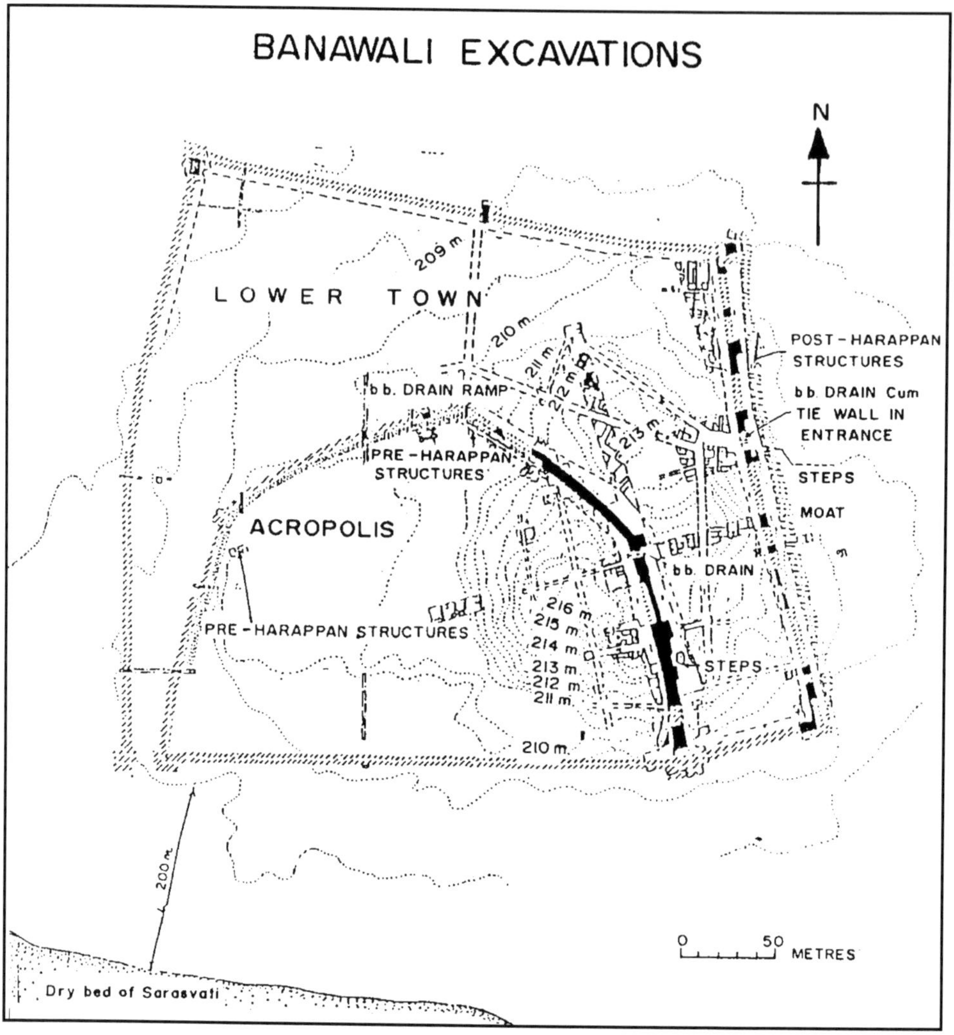

Fig. 3.4. Banawali Excavations.

bank of the now-dry Chautang, anciently known as the Dṛiṣadvatī, a tributary of the Sarasvatī. It was doubtless one of the major Harappan settlements, covering over a hundred hectares (Nath 1998-99).

Seven different areas, named RGR-1 to RGR-7, were partly excavated. In RGR-1, besides the usual houses, laid out along the cardinal directions, an interesting structural feature was discovered. Located a little away from the

Fig. 3.5. Banawali: Section across the moat. Mature Harappan.

residential area, this structure was circular on plan, with two small semi-circular adjuncts, one each on the west and east. Altogether, it measured 5 m east-west and 2.92 m north-south, with a depth of 1.30 m. In the middle there stood two independent shafts, arch-like on plan and having a width of 46 cm. The side-walls of the entire complex, including those of the shafts, were burnt deep red, implying prolonged fire-activity. At the bottom there was also a 30-cm thick deposit containing charcoal and ash. While no pots were actually found inside this complex, it is not unlikely that it may have been used for firing small-sized pots which had anciently been taken out.

RGR-2 yielded some important information about the structural remains of the Mature Harappan times. In its southern part, two mud-brick platforms, riveted with kiln-fired bricks were identified. These were oriented along the cardinal directions. On their top there lay sacrificial pits and two 'fire-altars' containing clay stele and circular terracotta cakes. The two fire-altars were contiguous and behind them was a north-south wall, a situation similar to that at Kalibangan and implying that the worshippers had to face the east.

On the western side of this mound the remains of a fortification-wall were also discovered. Oriented in a north-south direction and made of mud bricks, it measured 12 m in width at the base. It is extant to a height of 3 m and the exposed length so far is 30 m. The bricks, which are of the standard Mature Harappan ratio, viz. 4: 2: 1, are placed in a stepped fashion in the successive courses, both on the interior and exterior, with the result that the wall slopes back as it rises upwards. In an area a little to the south the continuation of this wall also noted. Over here a construction of kiln-fired bricks seems to indicate a stepped entrance.

RGR-6, which is bereft of Mature Harappan remains, is a very good area for horizontal excavation of the Early Harappan remains. However, even the limited work that was carried out in this area revealed a 4.5-metre thick deposit of the Early Harappans. In the upper 2.5 m four structural sub-periods were encountered, below which, although no structures were met with in the limited dig, still there were ample indications of floors which evidently must have been associated with some buildings.

(IV) HARAPPA

In Sahiwal District of Pakistani Punjab, Harappa lay on the left bank of the Ravi river, which has since shifted its course way to the north. The site comprises at least three clear-cut mounds, named from north to south as 'F', 'AB' and 'E'. Of these, Mound AB is the highest and is thought to represent the 'Citadel', encompassed by a mud-brick wall, measuring 13.5 m in width at the base but tapering upwards. On the exterior there was a revetment of kiln-fired bricks, a little more than a metre at the base. In a trench cut across the western side, a 6-m high mud-brick platform was found juxtaposed to the back of the wall. On it six structural sub-phases were identified. Whether this platform ran through the entire Citadel, providing a base for the superstructures could not be ascertained because of the limited excavation in this trench, but elsewhere within the Citadel mud-brick masses were no doubt met with in earlier excavations (Kenoyer 1998, Vats 1940 and Wheeler 1947).

Among the more important structures discovered in Mound F particular mention may be made of a massive granary (Fig. 3.6). It had two blocks, one each on the east and west, with a passage in between. Each block consisted

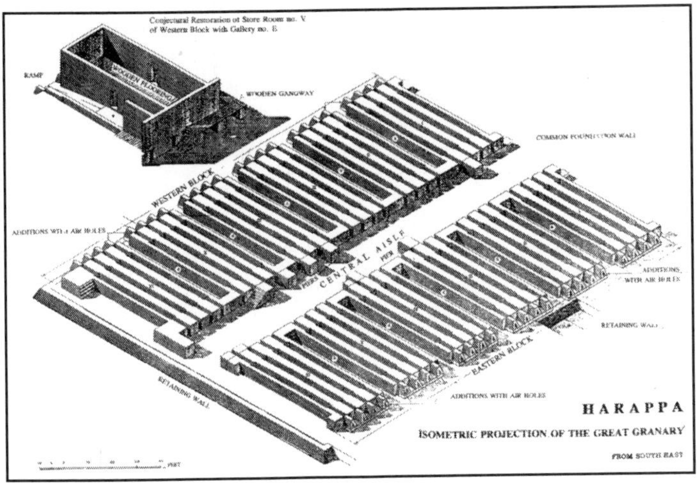

Fig. 3.6. Harappa: Isometric Projection of the Great Granary. Mature Harappan.

of six units, each unit measuring externally 15 x 6 m. In a recent dig at the northern periphery of this mound the remains of a thick mud-brick wall have been identified. If in future excavations this wall is traced around the entire mound, this area too would claim to have been fortified, like Mound AB. The other noteworthy structures in this area are: brick-on-edge platforms with a central hollow space, supposedly used for thrashing cereals; and workmen's quarters. The latter were constructed in a barrack-like fashion in two east-west rows, with a narrow gap in between. Each unit, measuring 17 x 7 m, comprised a room and a courtyard which had an oblique entrance.

Mound E, located to the south of Mound AB, would appear to be the 'Lower Town'. It had streets, lanes, regular residential houses and drains. Further, this area was also enclosed by a peripheral wall, which has been exposed to a length of over 25 m on the southern side and for quite some distance in the northeast. With a width of about 6-7 m, it is available to a height of 2.5 m. On the southern side there was a gateway, flanked by two piers made of kiln-fired bricks. The eastern part of this mound was used for industrial purposes, viz. for the manufacture of steatite disc-beads, shell objects and weights, as indicated by the occurrence of raw material and waste products.

The earliest occupation at Harappa began with what has been called by the excavator as the 'Ravi Phase', ascribable to circa 3,300-2800 BCE. In continuation, there are the Early, Mature and Late Harappan Phases, taking the story into the first half of the second millennium BCE. This last Phase is known as that of Cemetery H, characterized by a somewhat different kind of pottery having a bright red slip with paintings in jet-black pigment.

Human burials have been discovered in an area south of Mound AB and west of Mound E. Of these, the earlier ones relate to the Mature Harappan Period and the later to the Cemetery H. In the Harappan burials, the body was laid supine in a grave-pit, with the head towards the north. Some pottery and other goods were also placed in the grave. In Cemetery H, there were two kinds of burials. Whereas in the earlier ones the full body was buried in a pit, in the later only selected bones and the cranium were interred in large jars.

(V) MOHENJO-DARO

Though at present about 5 km away from the right bank of the Indus, in ancient times the settlement at Mohenjo-daro seems to have hugged the river. On plan, there are two major parts, a 'Citadel' on the west and a 'Lower Town' on the east, the overall perimeter being about 5 km.

Forming a rough rectangle and about 380 m north-south and 190 m east-west, the Citadel rises to a height of about 12m above the surrounding ground-level. Amongst the structures that lay within it the more noteworthy ones are: a bath, a granary and an 'assembly hall'. In the bath-complex, the tank proper measured 11.7 m north-south and 6.9 m east-west, with a depth of 2.4 m (Fig. 3.7). It was approached through two staircases, one each on the north and south. Around the tank there were pillared corridors, behind which were located several rooms, in one of which there was a well which supplied water to the tank. Every care was taken to make the tank water-tight, particularly by using gypsum mortar. For the discharge of water there was a large, corbelled drain in the southwest corner.

To the west of the bath there was the granary of which only the basal part now survives. Measuring 45 m east-west and 22.5 m north-south, it consisted of twenty-seven blocks of kiln-fired bricks, arranged in three rows of nine each. It

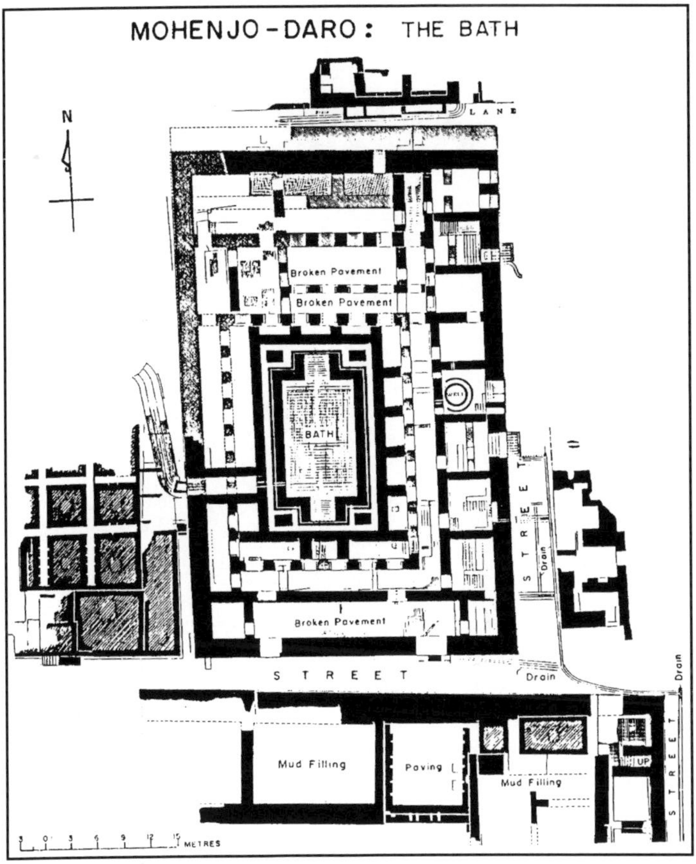

Fig. 3.7. Mohenjo-daro: The Bath. Mature Harappan.

appears that over these blocks there stood a superstructure of wood-work, which has since perished. The space in between these blocks provided passage for air so that the grain stored on the wooden floor of the granary could breathe and thus be saved from humidity.

In the southern part of the Citadel there was yet another important building. Measuring 27-m square on plan, it had twenty piers, laid in five east-west rows of four each. It has been surmised that this building may have functioned as an assembly hall for religious/secular purposes.

It is not clear if the Citadel at Mohenjo-daro was fortified, as was the case at Harappa and Kalibangan. However, the presence of a few towers along the periphery seems to suggest that there may have been a fortification-wall surrounding the Citadel. Only further excavation can settle the issue.

Running across the Lower Town there were at least two major north-south and an equal number of east-west streets, dividing it into nine major blocks. Each block was further subdivided into house-complexes by minor streets and lanes. Whereas the major streets were as much as 9 m in width, the lanes could be only 1.5 m. Through the streets was laid out an excellent underground drainage system, duly covered and provided with manholes at suitable places. As might be expected, the size and layout of the houses varied considerably. Thus, for example, one of the big houses measured 75 m across. It had two courtyards and around each courtyard there were living rooms. In the smaller of the courtyards there was a bread-oven and one begins to wonder if the rooms around the smaller courtyard were used by the ladies, as has been the practice in the houses of big landlords in many part of India even up to the recent times. An average middle-class house, on the other hand, was relatively small but certainly much bigger than the houses which evidently belonged to the labour-class. These last-named houses were indeed in the form of barracks, each tenement having only two small rooms. Within the township there were shops as well as workshops of potters, bead-makers, shell-workers, copper-smiths, etc. (Marshall 1931 and Mackay 1938.)

(vi) Surkotada

Located in the Kachchha region of Gujarat, Surkotada has yet another kind of town-planning. Here the Citadel and the Lower Town were juxtaposed to each other, with a common wall in between, which had an opening for intercommunication. Both the units were square on plan, each measuring 60-65 m internally. The overall orientation of the entire complex, as usual, was along the cardinal directions (Fig. 3.8). It is reported that whereas the structures in the Citadel were placed on platforms, there were no platforms beneath the houses in the Lower Town. Each unit had an entrance on the southern side, but while that to the Lower Town was a simple one, the one leading into the Citadel had a barbican, a ramp, steps and guard rooms. The

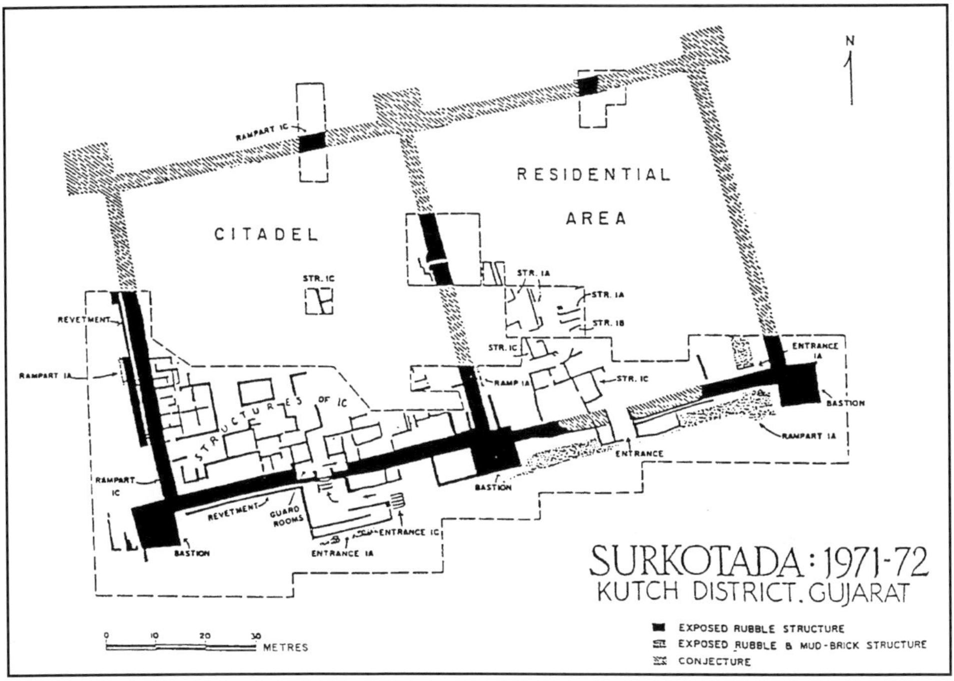

Fig. 3.8. Surkotada: Plan of the Harappan Settlement.

enclosure walls of both the units had a mud/mud-brick core with a veneer of stone-rubble which is available locally in plenty.

The site yielded the usual Harappan pottery and antiquities. However, of interest is the fact there also occurred a black-and-red ware with white-painted designs, which shows contacts with the Banas valley in Rajasthan, which is its home.

A very noteworthy discovery at Surkotada was that of the bones of the true horse (*Equus caballus* L.)whose association with the Harappan Civilization has been a matter of debate. We shall talk more about it in a subsequent chapter. (Joshi 1990.)

(VII) DHOLAVIRA

In the Kachchha region there is yet another site, called Dholavira. With its unique town-planning, use of stone-pillars in construction, the earliest known stadium, a remarkable system of water-supply, unusual graves and last

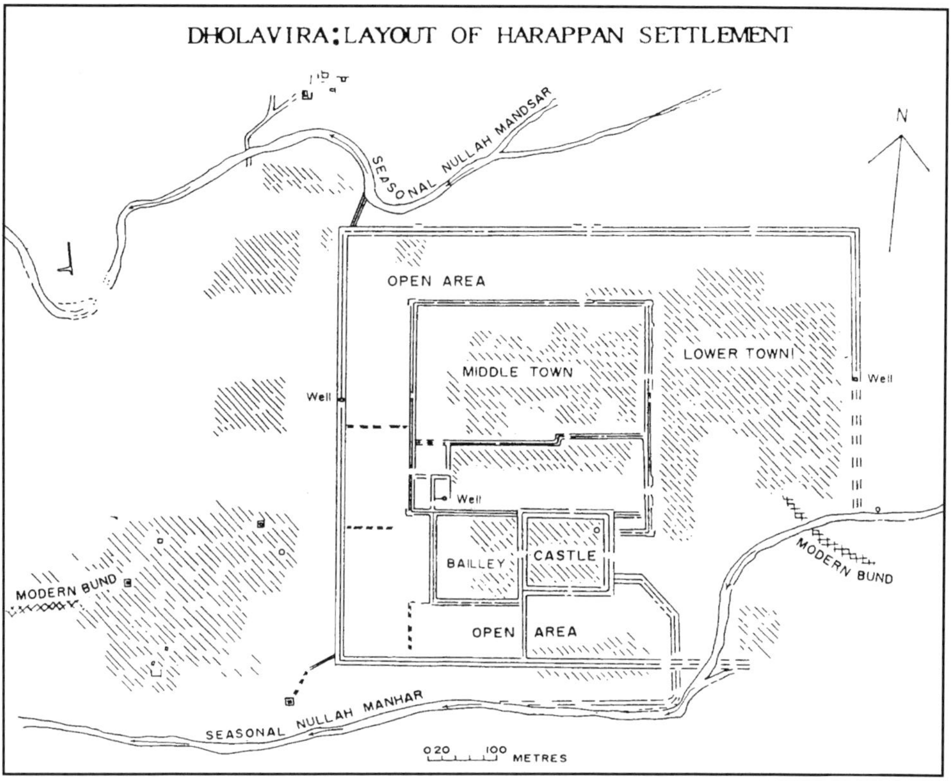

Fig. 3.9. Dholavira: Layout of the Harappan Settlement.

but not the least the largest inscription, it is decidedly one of the most impressive sites of the Harappan Civilization (Bisht 1991).

The settlement comprised a Citadel, a Middle Town and a Lower Town, all having their own enclosure walls yet interwoven into one complex (Fig. 3.9). Oriented along the cardinal directions and made of mud bricks with stone veneer, the outermost enclosure walls formed a rectangle on plan, covering an area of about 770 m east-west and 615 m north-south. On the exterior of these walls there were rectangular/square bastions at different points. Two seasonal nullahs flowed past this enclosure, named Mansar and Manhar, respectively on the northern and southeastern sides. The Dholavira engineers harnessed the waters of these nullahs for the use of the inhabitants.

The Citadel-complex, fortified and oriented along the cardinal directions, consisted of two conjoined units, more or less of equal size. Called respectively 'Bailey' and 'Castle' by the excavator, these units were interconnected by a gate passing through the medial wall. The nature of the structures in these two parts, however, differed, reminding one of a similar situation in the Citadel at Kalibangan. The Bailey seems to have had a residential character, since within it many houses have been found. Also, there was a structural complex comprising four juxtaposed underground chambers, lined with stones and each measuring approximately 3 x 3 m on plan and 2.6 m in depth. It is likely that these chambers were used for the storage of grains, though no grains as such were actually found.

The Castle, however, presented a different kind of scenario. From its western gateway, there ran a 13-m wide street, leading to the opposite gateway. It divided the Castle into two major parts, northern and southern. While the picture of the structures in the northern parts is still unclear, in the southern part a major water-related complex has been identified. There was a stoned-lined well, with an internal diameter of 4 m. It has been excavated to a depth of 13 m, without reaching the bottom. Abutting the edge of the well, there was a trough with a stone slab at the base and three vertical slabs on each side (Pl. X). In the southwestern corner of the trough there was an aperture through which water went into a covered drain which, after some distance, fell into a stone-lined tank, measuring 4.35 x 2.95 x 3.58 m. It was provided with steps which led down to a stone-paved floor. Nearby there was yet another tank which, however, has not been fully exposed. This complex at Dholavira reminds one of a more or less similar set-up in the Citadel at Mohenjo-daro, and naturally one begins to think in terms of a ritualistic context. Another noteworthy feature within the Castle was a large-sized drain which, passing through the major street, cascaded into the Bailey, finally to discharge into the open area outside.

The wall around the Castle stands even now to a height of 9 m. It had a basal width of 18.5 m and was made of mud bricks with a veneer of stones. Besides the western gate, interconnecting the Bailey and the Castle, there were three

Fig. 3.10. Dholavira: Inscription, consisting of ten Harappan signs.

more gates, one each on the north, east and south, of which those on the north and east have been excavated. Both these were laid out through the thickness of the enclosure wall and had a long flight of steps which descended to the floor of a passageway on the exterior. On either side of this passage there were chambers and in the front an open terrace. On the floor of one of the chambers in the northern gateway-complex a large-sized inscription comprising ten letters in the Harappan script has been found (Fig. 3.10). These letters had a height of 35-37 cm and width of 25-27 cm. and were made from carefully sliced pieces of some 'crystalline material, maybe rock, mineral or paste'. The excavator is inclined to think that it was some kind of a sign-board, put up at the gate.

In the side-chambers of the eastern gateway have been found parts of stone pillars, variously cubical, cylindrical and hour-glass-like in shape (Fig. 3.11). Some of these specimens still bear polish, and had not these been found *in situ* one would doubted that these really belonged to the third millennium BCE, since we have so far been familiar only with Mauryan polished pillars of the third century BCE.

On the north of the Citadel there was an open space which may have functioned as a stadium. And to the north of the stadium was the Middle Town (Fig. 3.9) which, like the Citadel, was provided with an enclosure wall, made of stones. Of its gateways, only the one on the eastern side has so far been excavated. It is about 3 m in width, with grooves in the vertical slabs to suggest the fixture of door-frames. On each side of the gate vertical stones were placed, which

Fig. 3.11. Dholavira: A view of the eastern gateway of the Citadel.

evidently acted as fender posts. The gate opened into an east-west street measuring about 5 m in width. Within the Middle Town there were many other north-south and east-west streets/lanes, variously 5.75 m, 2.6 m, 1.8 m and 1.5 m in width. The houses were fairly large, with provision for a courtyard, peripheral living rooms, bathrooms, etc. There was also a good drainage system.

To the east of the Middle Town was the Lower Town. The alignment of the major west-east street that ran up to the above-mentioned gate in the Middle Town was more or less followed by a street in the Lower Town, so that an easy access was available from one to the other. Cutting this street at right angles there were two major streets in the Lower Town, besides, of course, many other east-west and north-south streets/lanes. In one of the houses in the Lower Town there were a stone-paved bathroom and a stone-lined drain, besides a sullage-pit immediately outside. In another house dressed stones were used in the walls and an interesting point is that these stones measured 40 x 20 x 10 cm – exactly matching the standard size of the mud bricks. Some of the houses had storage jars and querns too. All said, the houses in the Lower Town did not in any way reflect a low economic level of the inhabitants.

To the west of the main settlement of Dholavira there was a cemetery, which yielded some new data, including the use of stone orthostats and capstones in the graves and the erection of mud/mud-brick tumulus in a couple of cases. To these we shall refer while dealing later with the burial practices of the Harappans.

Within the 12-m thick deposit in the Citadel area, seven stages of cultural development (numbered I-VII from bottom upwards) have been identified. Of these, the first two stages may be regarded as pre-Mature Harappan, though in them such elements as the dish-on-stand, perforated jars, terracotta 'cakes', bricks in the ratio of 4: 2: 1were met with. However, seals and weights and most of the other typical Mature Harappan pottery-forms made their appearance only in Stage III. An interesting point has been observed by the excavator, R.S. Bisht, regarding the seals. In Stage III these bore animal figures, but no inscriptions, the latter appearing only in Stage IV. This Stage, with a thickness of about 5.5 m, represented the Mature Harappan Period in its full bloom. Then followed the decline, which is reflected in the loss of civic control and architectural degeneration in Stage V. At this point the site was abandoned for a while. When the site was re-occupied in Stage VI, there were some conspicuous differences. For example, the seals were now without animal figures, although the weights continued. There were some changes in the pottery-forms too, besides the appearance of a new ceramic, viz. a black-and-red ware. Once again there was a desertion. Separated by a time-gap, Stage VII is marked by a few noteworthy changes. Thus, in spite of a continuity in some pottery forms and small finds, the houses were now hut-like, circular and much smaller; also there was no drainage. A major decline had set in.

(VIII) LOTHAL

Located in Ahmedabad District of Gujarat, Lothal has given to the world the earliest dockyard, dating back to about the mid-third millennium BCE (Figs. 3.12 and 13). In antiquity, a river used to pass by the settlement at Lothal. This river joined the Bhogavo, which in turn met the Sabarmati, the last-named falling in the Gulf of Khambhāt, an inlet of the Arabian sea. Thus, there was a continuous riverine connection between Lothal and the sea. Sited immediately

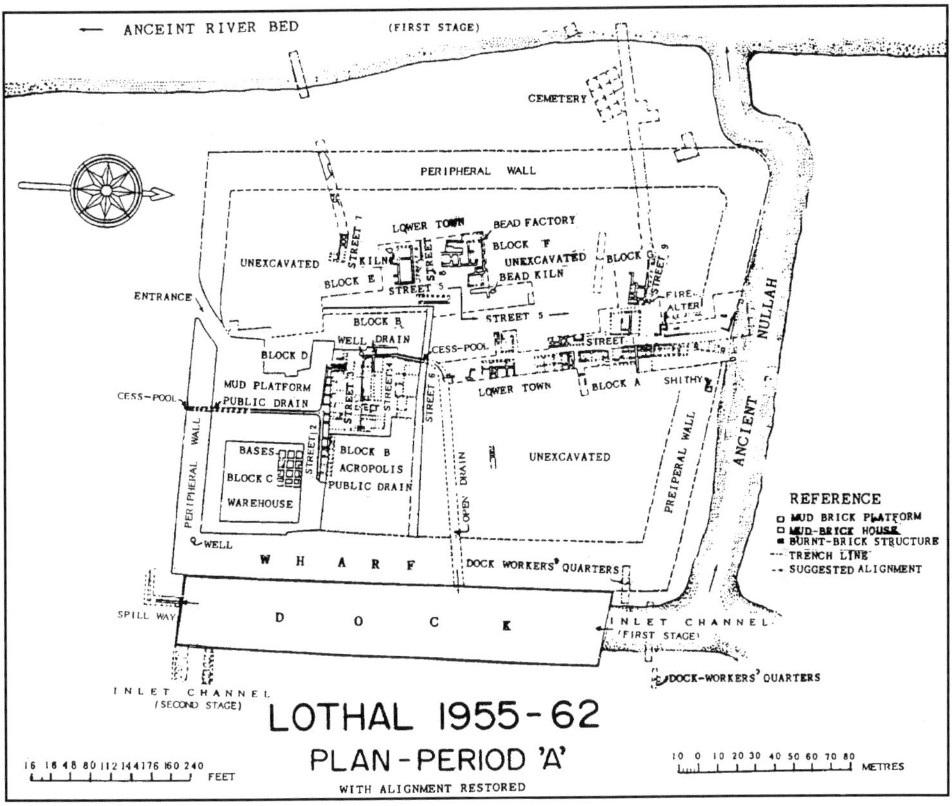

Fig. 3.12. Lothal: Plan of the Harappan Settlement.

to the east of the township, the dockyard formed a trapezoid on plan, with the longer axis north-south. Its retaining walls, made of kiln-fired bricks, measured in length, clockwise from the west, 215 m, 37 m, 212 m and 35 m respectively. In width, these were 1.5-1.8 m at the base, but tapered upwards to only 1 m. The maximum available height is 3.3 m, though originally these must have been much higher. (Rao 1979 and 1985)

There were two openings in the walls of the dockyard, allowing entrance/exit of the incoming and outgoing boats. One of these, measuring 12 m in width, was in the northern arm, while the other was through the eastern arm, having a width of only 7 m. It appears that the former was used in the earlier stages, while the other later on when the adjacent river shifted its course. In the southern wall there was a stepped exit through which the excess water drained out. The

Fig. 3.13. Lothal: The Dockyard. Mature Harappan.

functioning of the dockyard seems to have been somewhat as follows.

Taking advantage of the high tides in the sea, which had their impact way up on the connected water-courses, the cargo-loaded boats moved upwards and reached the dockyard. These were duly parked there, as indicated by the occurrence of stone anchors. The goods were unloaded on the adjacent wharf. Meanwhile, the commodities ready to be exported were taken out of the nearby warehouse and brought to the wharf to be loaded on the boats which were readied for the return journey to the sea. This trip was undertaken when another tide, reaching the dockyard, was on the wane, making it easier for the boats to follow it back to the sea.

The warehouse referred to above was constructed on a mud-brick podium, measuring 40 x 40 m on plan and 4 m in height. On it there stood a series of parallel mud-brick blocks, each measuring 3.6 x 3.6 x 0.9 m and separated one from the other by a 1.2m-wide passage (Fig. 3.14). The discovery of burnt wood and charcoal pieces in the passages suggests that the superstructure of the warehouse was that of wood. Equally noteworthy is the fact that from within these passages as many as sixty-five burnt clay sealings have been found. These have on one side the impressions of woven fiber and knotted cord and on the other of typical Harappan seals. This clearly shows that at the time the warehouse caught fire there lay in it packages duly sealed and ready to be exported. In the context of sea-trade, it must also be mentioned that at Lothal itself has been found a seal of the

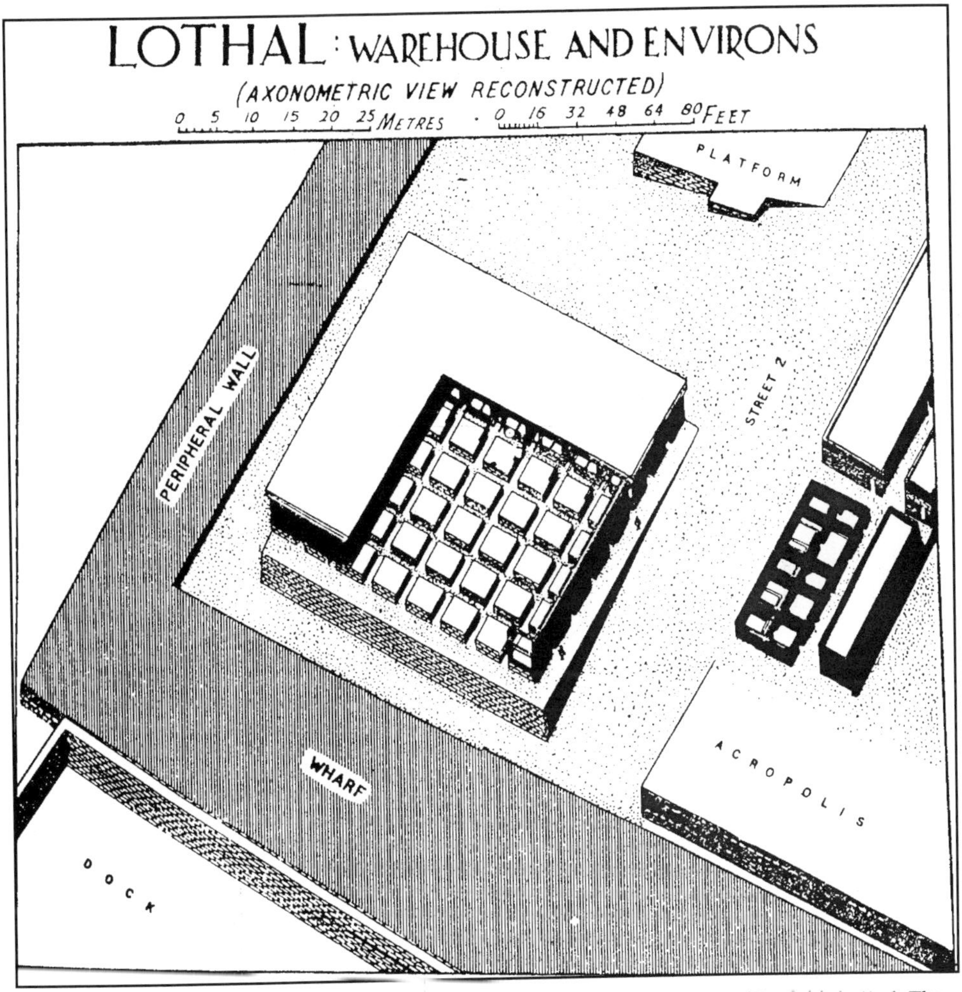

Fig. 3.14. Lothal: The Warehouse and Environs. Mature Harappan.

typical 'Persian Gulf' style, pointing to the identity one of the trade-partners. The exports from Lothal surely included etched carnelian beads, which were a hot favourite in western Asia, as evidenced by their occurrence at a number of sites in ancient Iraq and Iran.

The layout of the settlement at Lothal was different from that at the various sites discussed earlier. Over here the 'Citadel' was not a separate identity, as at Mohenjo-daro, Harappa and Kalibangan, but formed a part of the general township. However, the distinguishing feature between the

Citadel and the Lower Town at Lothal was that the former lay in an exclusive area on a 3.5-m high mud-cum-mud-brick platform. On plan, the platform was trapezoidal, the sides, in a clock-wise manner from the west, measuring 118 m, 125 m, 118 m and 113 m respectively. On it there stood a series of large-sized houses, a well, a row of twelve bathing floors, and concomitant drains discharging into a bigger one. The row of the bath-pavements brings to mind the complexes at Mohenjo-daro and Kalibangan. Was the Citadel at Lothal also used for some kind of religious purposes, housing priests in the aforesaid buildings? To the southeast of these houses was the warehouse referred to earlier.

The entire settlement, inclusive of the Citadel-complex, was enclosed by a mud and mud-brick wall having an average thickness of 12-13 m and extant height of 1.8-2.4 m. On plan, it formed a rough rectangle, oriented along the cardinal directions and measuring approximately 280 m north-south and 225 m east-west (Fig. 3.12). Piercing the southern wall there was an oblique entrance. The streets within were oriented along the cardinal directions, the widest and narrowest measuring respectively 12 m and 3.6 m. The houses had the usual plan: a courtyard surrounded by rooms on three sides, and an entrance on the fourth. Fire-altars too have been noted in some of the houses. The inmates were engaged variously in agricultural and industrial activities. The discovery of lots of beads in various stages of manufacture, of the raw material and even a kiln testifies to a thriving bead-industry at Lothal. Likewise, copper-artefacts were also manufactured locally, as evidenced by the discovery of ingots, crucibles, besides finished objects. Perhaps goldsmiths also constituted a part of the population. The site has yielded a large number of tiny gold beads and seven of a special type, viz. discular in shape with perforation along the diameter. While the other small finds included inscribed steatite seals, an ivory scale, an angle-measuring instrument, a terracotta figurine of a horse deserves special attention (Fig. 3.15).

On the northwest of the settlement, there lay the cemetery. Besides the usual single-burial graves, there were three which contained two skeletons each. More will be said about these when we discuss later the burial practices of the Harappans.

The occupational strata at Lothal, accounting for a total of 8.5 m, have been divided by the excavator into two Periods, named A and B. Period A has been further subdivided into four Phases, I-IV, and Period B has only one, viz. V. Thus, while Phase I represents just the beginning of the site, the township with its various nuances belongs to Phases II and III, the latter representing the peak. A kind of general downward trend is visible in Phase IV, while by Phase V the warehouse, dockyard and even the peripheral wall had gone into disuse. The township was ill-maintained and the drainage system had become defunct. Clearly, the curtain had been drawn on the glory that was Lothal.

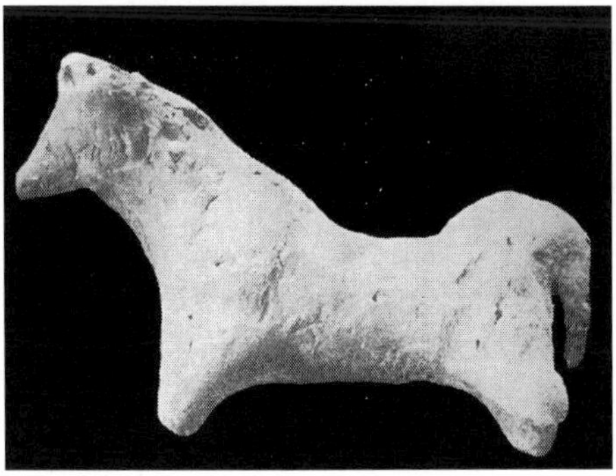

Fig. 3.15. Lothal: Terracotta Horse. Mature Harappan.

C. THE HARAPPAN ECONOMY

In the previous pages we have discussed in some detail the layout of a few important settlements of the Harappan people. Now we pass on to some other noteworthy aspects of their way of life.

(I) AGRICULTURE

Though today we may boast of the various industrial installations in our country, it cannot be denied that food-production still remains the backbone of our economy. And it was more so in the third millennium BCE when industrial revolution was a long way away. Wheat and barley were the main crops raised by the Harappans. Of the former, at least three varieties have been discovered, viz. the club wheat (*Triticum compactum*), the Indian dwarf wheat (*Triticum sphaerococcum*) and *Triticum aestivum.* As regards barley, besides the six-rowed variety (*Hordeum vulgare*), which preponderated, *Hordeum sphaerococcum* and *Hordeum vulgare nudum* have also been identified. While these cereals constituted the mainstay in the Indus and Sarasvatī valleys, in the southwestern domain of the Harappan Civilization, particularly in the Saurashtra region of Gujarat, millets seem to have been the favourite. At Rojdi the following have been identified: *rāgī* (*Eleusine* sp.), *kodon* (*Paspalum scrobiculatum*), *ṣawā* (*Enchinochloa colonum*) and *jowār (Sorghum)*. Lothal too has yielded millets, for example *kāngnī* (*Setaria italica* Beauv). Of rice too, the evidence is emerging. Whereas at Lothal and Rangpur its husk and spikelets were found mixed with clay-lumps, Hulas has yielded actual grains, though no doubt the context is Late Harappan. The Harappans also grew sesame and mustard which may have been used for preparing oil. However, the most noteworthy is the cultivation of cotton, of which no evidence is yet available from other contemporary civilizations. In fact, Mehrgarh, on the Indian subcontinent, takes the cultivation of cotton back to the fifth millennium BCE.

That the Harappan food-economy was in the surplus is clearly indicated by the large, highly organized granaries discovered at Mohenjo-daro and Harappa. At Dholavira too a series of juxtaposed, stone-lined, underground chambers are thought to have been used for the storage of grains. While these granaries may have functioned as special reserves under the control of some central authority, to be used on special occasions or in an emergency, even individual householders had their own arrangements for storage of grains, as indicated, for example, by the presence of a number of large-sized jars in one of the rooms in a house in the Lower Town at Kalibangan.

Some of the other items which the Harappans added to their dietary were: field peas, melon, dates, and bananas. They also grew grapes and hyacinth beans, and even raised esoteric plants like *henā* (*Lawsonia inermis*) whose leaves are pounded and used even today for colouring palms and nails. Mention may also be made of jasmine (*Jasminum* sp.) and *pārijāta* (*Nyctanthes arbortristris*) whose excellent fragrance must have kept the Harappans in good cheer.

(II) Animal Husbandry

While assessing the economic wealth, the input of animal husbandry is often underrated, even though it is well known that there are many countries, even in the present industrial age, where animals constitute the primary or a major source of wealth. To the Harappan economy too the animal world had indeed a lot to contribute. The people domesticated the humped bull (*Bos indicus* Linn.), as well as the humpless variety. These seem to have been used variously for ploughing the agricultural fields as well as for transporting men and material, in the latter case by harnessing them in carts. The cow was a good source of milk and a variety of milk-products, such as curds, butter-milk and clarified butter (*ghee*). Then there were the sheep (*Ovis orientalis vignei* Blyth) and goat (*Capra hircus asgrus* Erxleben) which too must have yielded milk, besides providing meat. The sheep was a source of wool (*ūrṇā*) as well. The pig (*Sus scrofa cristatus* Wagner) was also domesticated, both for food as well as for scavenging. Besides, wild animals, such as the spotted deer (*Axis axis* Erxleben), blackbuck (*Antelope cervicapra* Linn.), and *sāmbhar (Cervus unicolor Kerr)* were also hunted for food. This is indicated by the cut and charred bones of the aforementioned animals. The fish and turtle were also consumed as a part of the dietary. Of the former, many varieties have been found in the occupational debris: e.g. the *rohu* (*Labeo rohita*), *shingarī* (*Mystus aor, M. seenghala*), *khagga* (*Rita rita*), etc. There is also evidence for the domestication of the camel as well as the elephant. While the former was useful in transportation, particularly in the desert areas, the latter may have been useful in many ways: not only in the uprooting and transportation of trees for fire-wood, but also by providing the rare and costly item, namely the ivory.

Now to the horse (*Equus caballus* Linn.). While its association with the Harappan Civilization has long been a matter of debate, it has got to be emphasized that the evidence is mounting about its presence at Harappan settlements. Way back, in his excavations at Mohenjo-daro, Mackay found a terracotta figure of the horse. Recently a terracotta horse has also been found at Lothal (Fig. 3.15). However, besides these representations in terracotta, actual bones of the animal have been found at a number of sites, such as Lothal, Kalibangan and Surkotada. Writing about the evidence from the last-named site, the internationally renowned archaeozoologist from Budapest, Professor Sandor Bokonyi, states: 'The occurrence of true horse (*Equus caballus* Linn.) was evidenced by the enamel pattern of the upper and lower cheek and teeth and by the size and form of incisors and phalanges (toe bones).' This animal must have been of immense use in speedy travel as well as in the transportation of goods.

(iii) Marine, Mineral and Forest Resources

The Harappan Civilization was not land-locked. It also had the advantage of a fairly long coastline along its southern fringe – from Gujarat, via Sindh to Baluchistan. Thus, sea-food must have supplemented that from the inland rivers. However, the exploitation of chank shell (*Xancus pyrum* Linn.), of which there is ample evidence, must have helped the economy quite a bit. Inlays, bangles and other ornaments were made from it, not only for home consumption but also for export. Above all, the availability of a long coastal stretch, with appropriate sheltered bays, helped a great deal in safely pursuing sea-borne trade with the contemporary western world, to which we shall refer a little later.

The mountainous regions within the Harappan domain were duly exploited for the procurement of necessary stones and minerals. It seems that the Sukkur-Rohri hills were the prime source for the supply of chert of which a variety of small tools, such as borers, blades and arrowheads, were made. Likewise, some varieties of semi-precious stones for bead-making, e.g. agate, carnelian, etc., were obtained from Gujarat. But certain other semi-precious stones had to come from long distances. It is not unlikely that the Harappan settlement of Shortughai in far off Afghanistan may have been motivated, amongst other things, by a desire to exploit the local lapis lazuli mines. Some of it may have also come from the Chagai hills in Baluchistan. Turquoise too had to be brought from a long distance. The source of copper seems to have been the Khetri-Ganeshwar mines in Rajasthan, while lead may have been obtained from Ajmer in the same region. For the yellow metal – gold, the Harappans had to look southwards, to Kolar and other mines in Karnataka.

The forest resources were equally important to the Harappans. For firing billions of bricks, as encountered at Mohenjo-daro, Harappa, Lothal and other sites, they needed plenty of wood. The supply in the immediate neighbourhood being insufficient, far-off forests had to be exploited. And for certain specialized woods, the Harappans did not hesitate to venture into the Himalayan regions. It has been noted that the lid of a coffin discovered in one of the graves at Harappa was made of deodar (*Cedrus deodara* Loudon). The wood must have come from the aforesaid region. In fact, this discovery points to an important aspect of transportation.

Whereas in the case of the metals and minerals discussed above land-transport would have done the job, in that of bringing down the deodar to Harappa, all the way from the Himalayan region, the Harappans must have used the same method as is done even now, namely to float the logs of wood down the river and collect the same at relevant places downstream.

(iv) Certain Industries too

Besides agriculture and animal husbandry, certain industries too helped in the economic growth of the Harappans. These included bead-making, shell-working, ivory-carving, metal-smithy and so on.

Lothal and Chanhu-daro were great centres of **bead-making**. For example, S.R. Rao, the excavator of Lothal, records (1985: 580): 'A bead factory with a working platform in the open courtyard surrounded by eleven rooms has been laid bare in Block E near the acropolis. Two earthen jars, one containing 582 carnelian beads and another containing 212 beads of carnelian, shell and steatite, were found embedded in the platform. Several cores, flakes, ground and unbored beads were scattered all over the courtyard and in the rooms around. To the northeast of this factory is a kiln used for baking the raw material and finished product. ... a drill-bit of bronze used in boring stone beads was found near the factory.' In this context special mention must be made of etched carnelian beads which were a hot favourite even in foreign markets, as evidenced by their occurrence at a number of sites in ancient Iraq, Iran and Central Asia. As already mentioned in Chapter II, bead-making is a flourishing industry even today in this part of Gujarat.

Equally important was the **shell-industry.** As stated earlier, the coastal region from Gujarat to Baluchistan provided opportunities for the collection of sea-shells, in particular the chank (*śaṅkha; Xancus pyrum* Linn.). Many sites, like Lothal in Gujarat and Balakot in Sindh, have yielded unfinished and finished specimens attesting to the local manufacture of shell objects. These included bracelets, rings, pendants, beads, inlays and even bowls, knives and gamesmen. The finished objects were traded inland and even abroad.

Ivory-working was yet another specialized industry. Sites like Mohenjo-daro and Lothal have yielded ample evidence in this regard – from raw material to finished goods. These included combs, mirror-handles, hair-pins, antimony rods, ear-ornaments, gamesmen and even seals and scales. Discussing the evidence from Lothal, Rao (1985: 630) remarks: 'A small tapering rod of ivory on which stains of red ochre are seen at the tip must have been used for decorating lips or nail-tips. A chemical examination of the pigment reveals that a paint has been applied.'

The metal industry.– While copper and bronze were prolifically used, there is evidence of working in gold, silver and even lead. In order to harden copper, tin was often added to it. Various techniques were used: such as sinking, 'raising', cold working, annealing, lapping, closed casting and even *cire perdu* involving the 'lost wax' process.

The **copper/bronze** objects were put to a variety of use. Thus, to help them in agricultural operations, which included the cutting down of unwanted forest accretions, the Harappans made axes, adze-axes and sickles. Chisels, straight or curved saws, plainer-bits, drills and awls were used in carpentry. For fishing there were the inevitable fish-hooks. Hollow-based and tanged arrowheads and spearheads may have been used for hunting small and big games. These could have also been used in warfare, but let it at once be added that so far no shield, body-armour or helmet has been found to establish any war-like activity of the Harappans. Pots and pans were also manufactured in copper/bronze, which included *thālīs* (dishes), *hāṇḍīs* (carinated cooking pots), handled frying pans and drinking goblets. Then there were ladies' ornaments such as bangles, rings, ear-studs, hair-pins with single- or double-spiral heads. Object of toiletry included circular, tanged mirrors, antimony rods, and small, narrow-mouthed vessels for keeping collyrium. And lest the men feel bypassed, there were razors too. Mention must specifically made of a three-in-one gadget similar to the present one (Pls. VII and VIII) whose components are used respectively for removing unwanted hair from the inner side of the eyelids, for cleaning spaces between the teeth and for taking out wax from the ears.

Ornaments, as always, were made of **gold and silver**. Of the latter metal, a few vessels have also been found. The ornaments included a variety of beads, pendants, amulets, broaches, etc. Attention may, however, be drawn to a hollow conical ornament which is even now worn on by womenfolk in Rajasthan and Haryana on their head (Pls. VI and V).

As a source of extra wealth, the **ceramic industry** may not have played a significant role. Nevertheless it had an important part to play in the daily life of the people. Thus, there were the *hāṇḍīs* for cooking food, large but shallow bowls for holding the cooked food, cups and plates for eating and goblets for drinking water. Dishes- and cups- on-stand may have been used for laying the food on. Three-legged *pātā*s were used for rolling the bread. Large jars, often with a narrow bottom, were fixed into the ground for storing grains. Medium-sized S-shaped jar, often painted on the exterior, may have been used for the storage of some special items. The excavations have also yielded perforated, cylindrical jars whose actual use remains unexplained.

The clay used for the preparation of the pottery was usually fine and well levigated. The pots were thrown on a fast wheel and were well fired. Often a reddish slip was applied over which designs were executed in black pigment. These included characteristic motifs such as the banana-leaf, pipal-leaf, peacock, fish-scales, intersecting circles, chess-board and so on. Human and animal motifs were few and far between. However, some specialized scenes call for attention. Thus, from Lothal come two pots on one of which is depicted the story of 'The Thirsty Crow' and on the other that of 'The Cunning Fox' (see Figs. 2.19 and 2.20).

(v) Trade and Commerce

While undoubtedly agriculture, animal husbandry, exploitation of natural resources and various industries lay at the base of the economic growth of the Harappans, it was trade that boosted it further. The Harappans were actively engaged in trade – both internal as well as external. In previous pages we referred to some of the centres where beads or shell and copper objects were manufactured. But there were many more. It was from such centres that the commodities concerned were traded out. This may have been done either directly through a trader hailing from the consumer-end or, more likely, through a network in which middle men played a vital part. However, we have yet to work out this mechanism in some detail and more particularly the routes followed by the traders within the Harappan domain. In so far as the external trade is concerned, we have a reasonably good picture of the sea-route and to some extent of the land-route as well.

The sea-trade was essentially along the coast since in those days high-sea navigation was unknown. Thus, ships starting from the Gulf of Khambhāt moved along the Gujarat coast, calling at ports like Bet Dwarka. Thereafter these entered the coastal regions of Sindh and Baluchistan where ports like Allahdino and Sutkagen-dor were available. Proceeding further west, the ships reached the Gulf of Oman, which provided halting stations (Fig. 3.16). In this area, a revealing fact has come to light. Excavation at Ra's a-Hadd has shown that out of the recovered pottery, as much as 98 per cent was Harappan. In other words, here was a colony of Harappan sailors.

From Oman the ships entered the Persian Gulf wherein the island of Bahrain was a very important trading station. Here a team of Indian archaeologists discovered a steatite seal which presents a good synthesis of the Harappan and Persian Gulf styles. In Mesopotamia, many sites, such as Tell Asmar, Tepe Gawra, Kish, Lagash and Ur have yielded objects of Harappan origin. These include etched carnelian beads, dice, terracotta figurines and objects of conch-shell and ivory, found in strata assignable to circa 2500-1800 BCE. In this context it needs to be added that Sargon of Akkad (circa 2350 BCE) records that in the harbour of his capital were berthed boats from Dilmun, Magan and Meluhha, which have been identified respectively with the Failaka-Bahrain region, Oman-and-southeast Arabian region and the Harappan Civilization zone.

The overland trade was with Iran on the one hand and with central Asia on the other. Some of the sites from where Harappan material has been discovered in Iran are Tepe Yahya, Shahdad, Hissar and Shah Tepe. Of the central Asian sites which traded with the Harappans particular mention may be made of Altyn Depe, Namazga and Khapuz. The Harappan material found at the central Asian sites includes the usual beads, elongated ivory dice, copper spearheads, handled frying pans, even some pottery such as the perforated jar, cylindrical vases and ring-stands and, last but not least, a stone seal bearing two signs in the Harappan

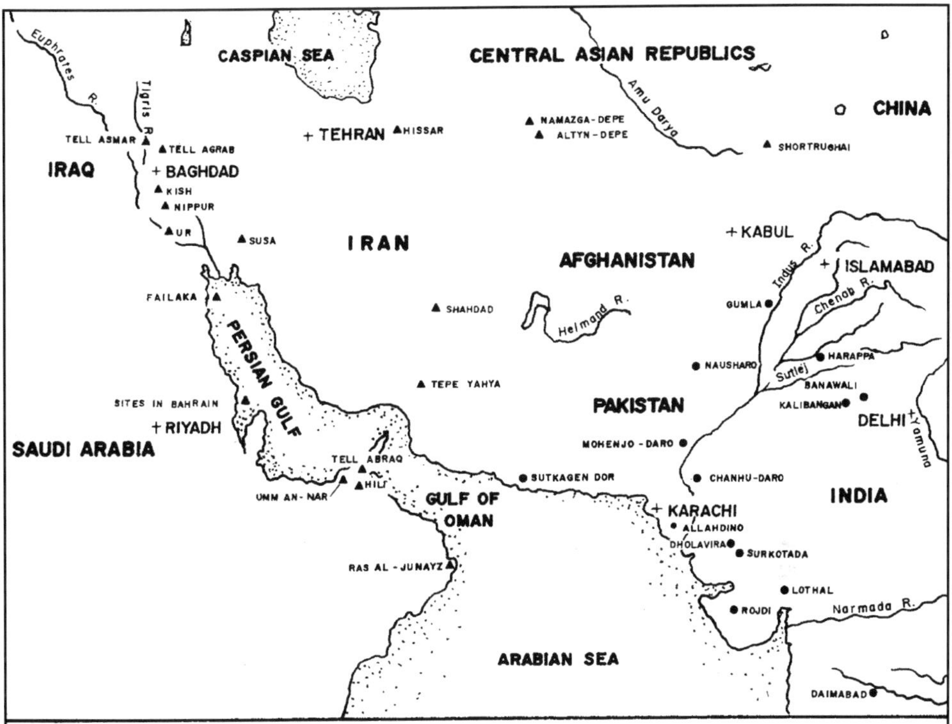

SOME SITES WITH HARAPPAN ARTEFACTS (Outside the Homeland) ▲

Fig. 3.16. Some Sites with Harappan artefacts (Outside the Homeland).

script and a silver pendant depicting a three-headed animal which is conceptually similar to that found on the Harappan seals.

In the basin of the Amu Darya and its left-hand tributary Kokcha, there lies a full-fledged Mature Harappan site, namely Shortughai. Covering an area of about 2.5 hectares, it has a 2.5-3 m-thick occupational deposit. This site may well have functioned as an intermediary trading depot between the Harappan mainland and central Asia, besides being a seat for the procurement of lapis lazuli from the nearby mines.

Trade, which was not mere barter, required at least four supporting tools, namely weights and measures, respectively to weigh and measure the goods sent out or brought in, seals to mark out the packages and a script to keep a record of the transactions.

Made usually of chert, but sometimes of jasper and agate as well, the weights were cubical in shape. While the smallest unit was of 0.871 grammes, evidently used for weighing precious items like gold, the highest recorded was 10865 grammes which may have been used for weighing grains and other heavy material. These weights followed an upward ratio of 1, 2, 8/3, 4, 8, 16, 32, 64, 160, 200, 320, 640, 1600, 3200, 6400, 8000 and 12,800. As regards the units of linear measurement, it is difficult to arrive at any final conclusion, since unfortunately all the four scales, discovered one each at Mohenjo-daro, Harappa, Kalibangan and Lothal, are incomplete (broken) and hence the markings on them cannot be categorically assessed. The material used for making these scales varied: ivory, bronze, shell and even clay. About seals and the script we shall talk a little later.

D. THE HARAPPAN ART

Various media were used by the Harappans to give expression to their artistic tastes. These included clay, metal and stone.

(I) In Clay

Made of finely levigated and well fired clay, the Harappan terracotta figurines represent humans as well as animals. Of the human figurines, the female ones are relatively elaborate. These have a thin waist but broad hips with a loin-cloth and girdle. The mouth is usually slit, the nose is pinched up while the eyes are indicated by small round pallets. They often wear necklaces and other ornaments and there is a fan-shaped head-gear as well. Some female figurines, painted in three colours, call for special attention. Their ornaments are painted in yellow, indicating that the same were made of gold. The hair is painted black, which is its natural colour. But what is most striking is that the medial partition line of the hair is painted red – something which at once reminds one of the practice of applying vermilion in the medial hair-line (called *sīmanta* or *māṅga* in Hindi) by Hindu women, as a symbol of their marital status (see Pls. I and II).

The animal figurines include the bull, elephant, rhinoceros, pig, monkey, dog, etc. Some of the bulls are to be noted for their forceful, dashing portrayal. A few dogs wear a collar (Fig. 2.10), while in the case of the monkeys some are so designed that these could move up and down a string. There are also examples of birds placed in a cage (Fig. 2.11).

(II) In Metal and Stone

When the people are well off, they naturally begin to think in terms of a somewhat luxurious living, including the production of what are known as objet d'art. So did the Harappans. They used both metal and stone for the purpose. While dealing with the various techniques employed by the Harappans for preparing their metal objects, we referred in passing to the famous bronze figure of the 'dancing girl' from Mohenjo-daro (Pl. III). Such is the charm of this mere 11-cm tall woman that she has rightly been regarded as one of the masterpieces of the Harappan art. The ankles and feet are missing from this figure, but there is another specimen from Mohenjo-daro itself having (unfortunately only) these parts wearing anklets, as if to validate her 'dancing girl' aspect.

Art in copper/bronze was not limited to human figures. It embraced the animal world too. These included, besides the elephant, dog, swan, etc., two most lively and forceful representations, viz. those of a short-horned humpless bull from Kalibangan (Pl. XXII) and a buffalo from Mohenjo-daro.

Stone was another medium which the Harappans used to express their artistic sensitivity. From Mohenjo-daro comes the well known figure, often called the 'priest king' or simply 'priest' (Pl. XII). About 18 cm in height and comprising only the upper part of the body, it is carved out of limestone. It has introvert eyes, suggesting a meditative pose, and wears a shawl in a manner which is typical of the *pujārīs* (priests) in India even now. The shawl has to be noted for its trefoil pattern.

From Harappa come two figures, both less than 10 cm in height. One of these represents a naked youth with a well built body. It is incomplete, but what is to be noted is that it has three sockets, one in the neck and one on each shoulder. It is obvious that in the former socket the head was meant to be fixed and in the latter two the arms. The other figure is to be noted for its posture: its body is somewhat twisted, and one of the legs thrown sideways, as if in a dancing pose.

Some scholars are of the view that it is a precursor of the later-day Śiva Natarāja (Lord Śiva in a dancing pose).

Of the animals in stone, particular mention may be made of a composite figure from Mohenjo-daro – a seated bull with ram's horns and elephant's trunk. It may be added that the concept of composite animals is common on the steatite seals (discussed below). The recent dig at Dholavira has brought to light a life-size and very artistic representation of the mongoose.

(III) The Glyptic Art

The Harappan glyptic art far excels that from either Egypt or Mesopotamia. Made of steatite and measuring on an average about 2-3 cm-square, the Harappan seals bear engravings of a very high order. Indeed, one is overawed by the majesty of the humped bull, with a muscular yet graceful body, powerful expression on the face, tall incurved horns and a swinging dewlap (Fig. 3.17). With an average thickness of 50-60 mm, the seals have a convex, perforated knob on the reverse, which was evidently used for the insertion of a thread for suspension. Besides the bull, the seals bear the figures of other animals like the elephant, rhinoceros, buffalo, unicorn, etc. Then there are combinations: for example in one case the hind part is that of a tiger, the front of a ram/unicorn, the horns of a bull, the tusk and trunk of an elephant and a human-like face. Above the animals there is usually an inscription in the typical Harappan script.

Fig. 3.17. Mohenjo-daro: Steatite seal, with the figure of a humped bull and an inscription. Mature Harappan.

At many sites, clay lumps with impressions of such seals have been found, indicating that these were used primarily for sealing packages. On the underside of the sealings there are marks left by the packing material as well as by the thread used for tying up. A classic example of this is the discovery of 65 sealings from the warehouse at Lothal. However, there are some seals which probably had some kind of religious association, for example the one with the figure of Paśupati (Pl. XV) or another showing a deity in a pipal-enclosure with an animal ushered in for sacrifice and a series of seven figures in the register below (Pl. XVII).

E. SOME OTHER ASPECTS OF THE HARAPPAN CIVILIZATION

(I) THE DISPOSAL OF THE DEAD

The general mode of the disposal of the dead seems to have been burial. In a rectangular pit the dead body was laid supine in an extended position, the head being to the north. The dead sometimes continued to wear ornaments, such as necklaces, rings and bangles. Also, placed along the dead body were objects of toiletry such as mirror and antimony rod, and pots whose number could be as large as seventy. A belief in life after death seems to be suggested not only by the aforesaid grave-goods but also by the presence of fowl-bones indicative of food-provision and even of a lamp to provide light in the dark journey ahead. Sometimes the grave-pit was lined with bricks (Fig. 3.18), and in one case, at Harappa, a mud-brick tumulus was also erected over the grave. In a few cases the body had been placed in a coffin; and in one example (again, at Harappa) while the body of the coffin was made of rosewood the lid was that of deodar (*Cedrus deodara*), evidently procured from the Himalayan region.

While interring a single human body in one grave seems to have been the normal practice, there were exceptions too. For example, Lothal has brought to light, besides the usual single burials, three examples in which two bodies were placed side by side. It has been surmised that these may represent the practice of *satī* (the wife joining the husband in death). However, the physical anthropologists who have examined these skeletons do not agree amongst themselves about the identification of the sex of the skeletons and, therefore, it is difficult to establish that in each case there was a male and a female.

Kalibangan has brought to light another kind of enigmatic burial-practice. In this case no skeleton was encountered in any of the sixteen graves excavated: only one

Fig. 3.18. Kalibangan: Grave 29. Mature Harappan.

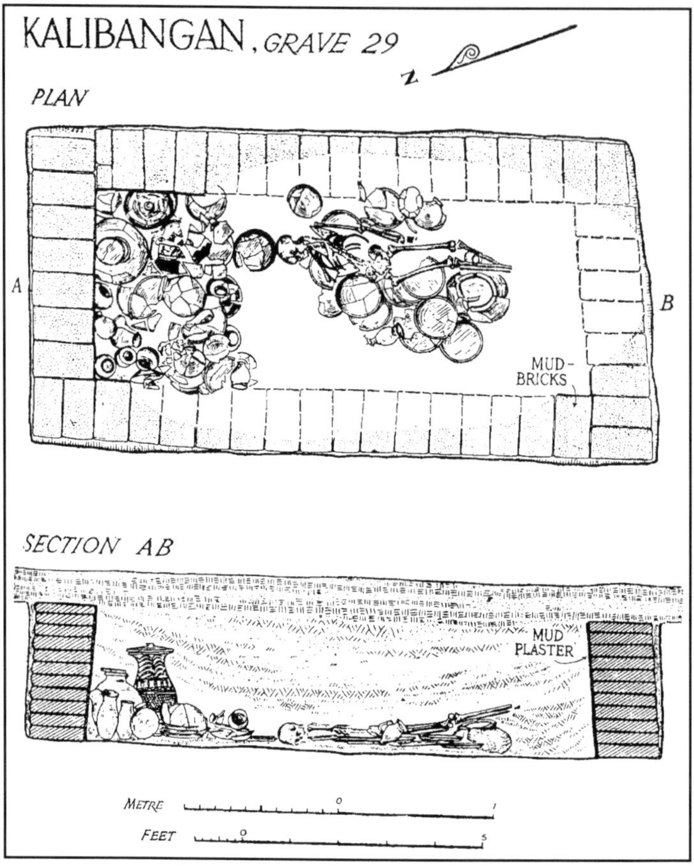

yielded a fragmentary piece of bone, whose exact identity also could not be established. On plan, these graves were not rectangular, like the usual ones, but were circular or ovoid. However, since these lay well within the cemetery complex their funerary association cannot be denied. Also, these graves had articles usually met with in the rectangular ones, such as pottery, beads, copper rings, etc. Amidst the pots interred in these graves, there always was a large jar occupying a prominent position. It was thought that this might contain ashes/charred bones in case these were post-cremation burials. But expectations were belied. However, if the interment was that of only ash sans bones, the same could have got so much mixed up with the earth inside the jar that its identification was not easy. In the alternative, could these have been just 'symbolic burials' for those who may have died elsewhere? Anyway, further investigation is called for.

Dholavira has thrown up yet another feature. Though the graves contain the human body as usual, these are lined with stone slabs and often have a capstone and/or stone rubble at the top. However, if we look back at the Harappan or Kalibangan graves, we would recall that there too the pits were sometimes lined with mud bricks, and at Harappa there also was a mud-brick tumulus to mark out the grave. Since at Dholavira stone was available in plenty, it may well be that the stone-slabs (orthostats) on the sides and the capstone-cum-rubble at the top represent merely a change from one material to another (readily available at the site) and not any major conceptual departure.

(II) Religion

There are at least two aspects of religion: one is metaphysical or philosophical and the other practical or ritualistic. In the former the seeker wants to know: who am I? Am I the body alone or something beyond that? What is this 'Life-Force' within me? What is the relationship between my own self and the Universal Power known as God? And so on. In the latter case, the person performs a variety of rituals through which he propitiates 'gods' and hopes to better for himself this world as well as the next, which he has already taken for granted. Maybe the Harappans too had a similar bicameral approach, though not much can be said about the former. The metaphysical and philosophical aspects can best be gleaned from books, but in the case of the Harappans no such treatise is available and the little information that could, if at all, have been gathered from some of the inscriptions on the seals remains blocked because of our inability to read them. However, an indication about some kind of a practice which now we call 'yoga' is given not only by the yogic *āsana*s in which some of the terracotta figurines are depicted (Fig. 2.21) but also by the limestone statue of the 'priest' whose eyes are introvert and indicate a meditative pose (Pl. XII). Some two thousand years later the practice of *āsana*s as well as the methodology of *dhyāna* (meditation) were incorporated in the eight-fold (*aṣṭāṅga*) path enunciated by Patañjali in his *Yogasūtra*.

Śaivism in one form or another appears to have been prevalent during the Harappan times. This is suggested by the well known seal from Mohenjo-daro, which depicts a figure seated in an yogic posture on a dais (*chaukī*), surrounded by animals (Pl. XV). This figure has been taken to represent Śiva in his Paśupati (Lord of Animals) aspect. And this is not the only seal; there are many others that depict this very deity, with minor variations, of course. That the Harappans did really practise Śaivism is now duly confirmed by the discovery at Kalibangan of a terracotta representation of Śiva-*liṅga*-cum-*yoni* (Pl. XIV). Besides Śiva, a few other deities also seem to have been worshipped. For example, a seal (Pl. XVII) depicts in its upper register a female figure within a pipal-enclosure and in front of it there are a kneeling devotee and a ram, the latter perhaps meant for offering. There are seven other figures (worshippers?) in a row in the lower register. The presence of a cult of the Mother Goddess is also suggested by a large number of terracotta figurines.

At least two types of rituals are indicated by the available evidence, one relating to 'fire-altars', and the other to animal sacrifice. In the houses in the Lower Town at Kalibangan usually one of the rooms was reserved for rituals connected with the 'fire-altars'. (These, however, are not to be confused with the fire-altars of the Parsis.) These altars were rectangular, measuring about 1 m x ½ m on plan, and were sunk into the ground to a depth of about 25 cm (Fig. 2.22). In the centre there stood a cylindrical or faceted clay stele, about 25-30 cm high, around which were placed circular-biconvex terracotta 'cakes', perhaps as 'offerings'. The presence of ash and charcoal testifies to the use of fire. While the 'altars' in the Lower Town were used by the householder concerned, the setting was quite different in the Citadel. As mentioned earlier, the Citadel was divided into two parts, a northern and a southern. While in the former there were residential houses, very likely of the priests, in the latter there stood individual platforms, each bearing a specific complex. Thus, on one of the platforms there was a row of seven fire-altars, with the aforesaid features of stele, 'cake' and charcoal (Fig. 2.23). In the front there lay embedded in the ground the lower half of a jar, full of ashes and charcoal. It is evident that in it fire was kept ready to be used in the altars. Behind the row of these altars there was a north-south wall, which suggests that anyone who used these altars had to face the east. Close by, on the north, there was a well along with a bath-pavement. This might indicate that anyone performing the ritual had to have a bath. In addition to Kalibangan, Banawali, Rakhigarhi, Lothal and Rangpur have also yielded the evidence of fire-altars. At Banawali, an apse-like enclosure wall surrounded the altar, and the excavator is inclined to think that the complex may have been some kind of an apsidal 'temple'.

A little away from the platform bearing the above-mentioned fire-altars there was another platform on which a sacrificial pit was located. Lined with kiln-fired bricks and measuring 1.25 x 1 m, it contained bovine bones and antlers, indicative of animal-sacrifice (Fig. 3.19). Evidence of animal-sacrifice has also been obtained from Rakhigarhi and Lothal. In this context, attention may also be drawn to an engraved terracotta cake found at Kalibangan itself. On one of its sides there is a man holding a rope which is tied to the neck of an animal. On the other there is a figure which may represent Śiva, as indicated by the head-gear. Put together, the two sides show how an animal was brought in for the sacrifice. Then there is a planoconvex terracotta tablet, found recently at Harappa. It depicts on the right a seated deity, in all likelihood Śiva, and on the left a man and a buffalo. The man holds one of the horns of the animal with his left hand, presses the head of the animal with his right foot and pierces the back of the animal with a spear held in his right hand. Evidently the scene seeks to portray the sacrifice of the buffalo in front of the deity (Pl. XVI).

(iii) The Script and Language

Right from the 1920s when the Harappan Civilization was discovered scholars have been attempting to decipher the script. Unfortunately, however, no one has yet hit the mark. According to some, like Asko Parpola, Walter A. Fairservis and I. Mahadevan, the language was Dravidian. On the other hand, S.R. Rao, M.V.N. Krishna Rao, N. Jha and others take it to be Sanskrit. In fact, a German scholar, Egbert Richter-Ushanas, goes to the extent of reading actual Vedic verses in some of the inscriptions. (I have not given bibliographical references to the authors mentioned above. However,

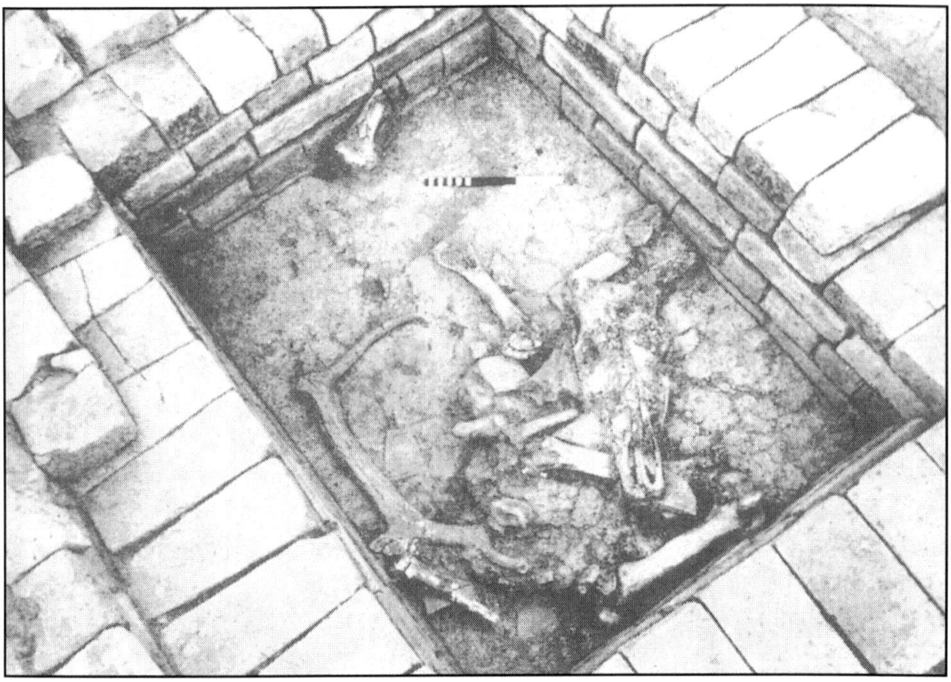

Fig. 3.19. Kalibangan: Brick-lined sacrificial pit. Mature Harappan.

interested readers may refer to Lal 1997 and Possehl 1996 in this regards.)

For any decipherment to be acceptable, it should fulfil at least the following few conditions. First, there should be a sound reason for assigning a particular sound-value to a given sign. Arbitrariness or 'intuition' is not the way. Secondly, once a particular sound has been assigned to a sign, it must be honoured all through the process of decipherment and not changed as per convenience of the decipherer. Finally, the resulting readings must follow the vocabulary and rules of the language arrived at, whether it is Dravidian or Sanskrit or yet some other language. It would not do to say that the language was 'some kind of proto-Dravidian or proto-Sanskrit, beyond the ken of any rules'. Thus, when put to the foregoing simple tests, all the above-mentioned attempts fail. Hence we are where we were in the 1920s.

Some features of the script can nevertheless be stated. It had long been argued whether the direction of writing in this script was from the right to the left or the other way round. A final seal to the debate was put by a couple of inscribed potsherds from Kalibangan where it was clear that the successive signs on the right were overridden by those immediately on the left, thereby establishing that the one on the right was written before that on the left (Fig. 3.20; Lal 1966). In other words, the direction of writing was from the right to the left. In case there was a second line in the inscription the style was boustrophedon, i.e. the second line was from the left to the right. This was perhaps found expedient since the first sign in the second line had to be in immediate continuation of the last one in the first line.

Fig. 3.20. Kalibangan: Inscribed potsherd. The overlap of letters shows that the direction of writing in the Harappan script was from the right to the left.

As to the nature of the script, viz. whether it was logographic, syllabic or alphabetic, available evidence tends to suggest that it may have most likely been of the second category. In a logographic script, like the Chinese, there is a sign for each word, thus letting the number of signs go up to tens of thousand. In a syllabic script, wherein a sign has a phonetic value and represents the combination of a couple of consonants along with a vowel, the number of signs considerably drops down. For example, the ancient Egyptian and Sumerian scripts, which were syllabic, had 100-150 signs. In an alphabetic language, each sign stands for a single sound, as in the case of the Devanāgarī or Roman scripts wherein the signs are respectively 48 and 26. In the case of the Harappan script the total number of signs still remains debated, since some of the signs appear to be a combination of two or even more signs. Thus, the estimates vary from 270 to 417. In all probability, therefore, the Harappan script may have been syllabic or syllabic-cum-logographic; in the latter case some of the signs may have stood for words.

It has been claimed by some scholars that the Harappan script was derived from one of the West Asian scripts, but there is no convincing proof of that. However, there is a greater possibility that it may have emerged on the Indian soil itself, since many of the signs in the monumental Mature Harappan script have morphological parallels in the graffiti on the Early Harappan pottery. In cases where there occur two or three signs in the Early context, it may well be that these had an 'inscriptional' status. It is also clear that the script far outlived the Mature stage and there are examples of it even in a Megalithic context dating as late as the first quarter of the first millennium BC. But once again, alas! the script has kept close to its chest all its secrets.

(IV) SOCIAL STRATIFICATION

Whether the Harappans were divided into some kind of a social hierarchy it is not easy to answer in the absence of any documentary evidence. Perhaps the short inscriptions on seals, pottery, etc. might have helped us in case these included, if at all, the caste-names or professional surnames of the persons concerned. Unfortunately, however, the script remains undeciphered. In such an event, one has to turn to other pieces of evidence and see if these can help.

We may recall that the settlement at Kalibangan comprised the Lower Town and the Citadel, both of which were duly fortified. In the Lower Town there were large houses with open courtyards for keeping cattle and had also facilities for the storage of grains. In many of the houses seals and sealings were also found. All this would indicate that therein lived a fairly well-to-do section of the society, engaged in agriculture and trade activities. Within the Citadel, the southern half had platforms on which were located ritualistic structures, while in the northern half there lived probably the priests who supervised/performed the rituals.

In marked contrast to both the Lower Town and the Citadel, there was an area that lay to the south of the latter. Not only was it not fortified but the houses therein were small. Further, in one section of it there lay a large amount of pottery and ashes indicating that hereabouts there were the houses of potters. It would thus appear that in this area there lived the less privileged, working class. Indeed, a similar story is told by the workmen's quarters and working platforms located in the shadow of the Citadel at Harappa. Recent excavations at Mound E at this site have brought to light another fortified area equivalent to the Lower Town at

Kalibangan. This kind of dispensation of the Harappan settlements would indicate that the inhabitants were divided into three classes – a priestly class, occupying the Citadel; an agricultural-cum-trading class occupying the Lower Town; and an underprivileged, working class living in small houses and serving the above-mentioned two categories. It is also not unlikely that in the course of time the Harappan priestly class may have given rise to the Brāhmaṇas, the agricultural-cum-mercantile class to the Vaiśyas, and the underprivileged working class to what came to be known the Śūdras. In this context it may be of interest to note that in the *Bhagvadgītā* (Chapter IV, Verse 13), Lord Kṛiṣṇa says:

Chāturvarṇyam mayā sṛiṣṭam guṇa-karma vibhāgaśaḥ,

which means 'the four *varṇa*s (categories) were created by me in accordance with the *guṇa*s (propensities) and *karma*s (duties) of the people'. It is thus clear that, to begin with, these categories came into being because of the nature of the work carried out by the people concerned and it was only at a later stage that these divisions got fossilized in the form of *jāti*s, perhaps because the respective professions were passed on from the father to the son, in a hereditary manner.

(v) Political Set-up

The immense territory covered by the Mature Harappan Civilization, the efficient manner in which the metropolitan cities were governed, the highly organized trade-mechanism represented by a uniform system of weights and measures, the use of a single script all over the area and so on naturally make one inquisitive about the nature of the administrative/political set-up in those days. But the answer is not easy since, once again, we do not have any written documents to enlighten us on the subject. Thus, what follows is nothing more than an attempt at imaginative reconstruction. Indeed, in the present state of our knowledge one guess is as good as any other.

To begin with, perhaps a few questions may be posed. Was there a Harappan Empire, administering from a **single** centre the vast area from Sutkagen-dor on the west to Alamgirpur on the east and from Manda on the north to Daimabad in the south? Or were there many 'States' located variously in the aforementioned area? In search of the answer it may be well worth while to have a look at the scenario that prevailed before the rise of the 'Mature' stage. During the Early Harappan times too the area occupied was more or less the same, as indicated by such far-flung sites as Balakot, Amri and Kot Diji in Sindh, Gumla and Rehman Dheri in the northwest, Harappa in Punjab, Gamanwala in Cholistan, Kalibangan in Rajasthan, Banawali and Rakhigarhi in Haryana, and Padri, Lothal, Dholavira, etc., in Gujarat. And the cultural level achieved by these Early Harappans was also of no mean order. They too had planned their houses and streets along the cardinal directions, laid a peripheral/fortification wall around some of their bigger settlements, standardized their bricks, were inscribing their pots with signs some of which may have given rise, at least morphologically, to certain signs of the Harappan script, were engaged even in long-distance trade as indicated by the presence at some of the sites of material such as turquoise, lapis lazuli, etc. Amidst a cluster of smaller settlements, some of the Early Harappan sites had also grown to a considerable size, for example Gamanwala in Cholistan was as large as 27.3 hectares. It would thus appear that even during the Early Harappan times some kind of hierarchy amongst the various sites had begun to emerge. Thus, a few sites may have 'dominated' the others in the neighbouring areas. In other words, some kind of political set-up may have already begun to emerge during the Early Harappan times. Maybe these were 'Chiefdoms' or even 'Early States'. Thus, it is not unlikely that the same scenario, of course with much more sophistication and refinement, may have persisted even during the Mature Harappan times.

It has often been argued that a uniformity of the material culture over such a vast area could not have been achieved unless it was enforced through the agency of an empire. But such a premise is basically faulty: 'empire' and 'cultural uniformity' are two different entities. For example, if we cast even a casual glance at a later-day scenario we find that around the middle of the first millennium BC, there existed a more or less uniform material culture all over northern India – from Taxila in the northwest to Tamluk in the east and to the Narmada valley in the south. It was distinguished, amongst other items, by the well known Northern Black Polished Ware, cylindrical weights of jasper/chert and

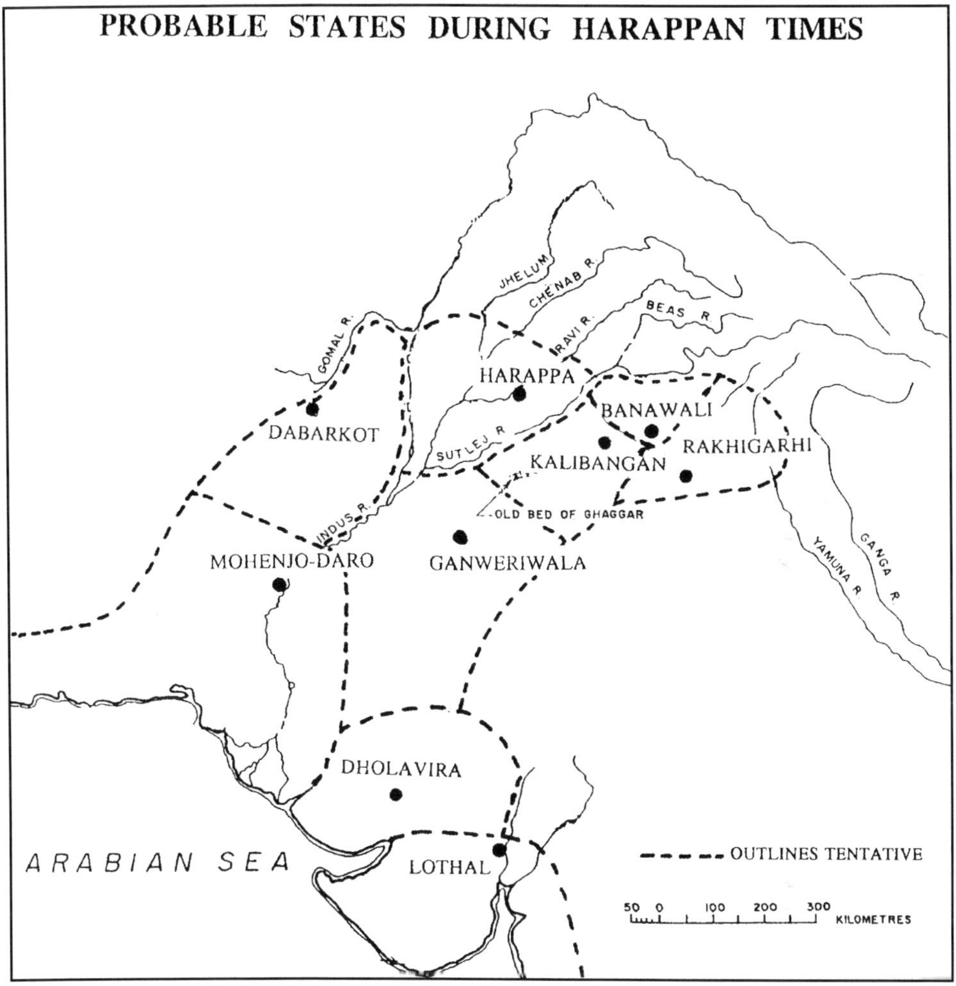

Fig. 3.21. Probable States during the Harappan times.

punched-marked and cast copper coins. At that point of time there was no empire. Instead, there were several States, viz. the *Ṣoḍśa Mahājanapadas*. Nothing precludes us from envisaging a similar situation during the Harappan times (Fig. 3.21).

Perhaps one may also mention here why the theory of a Harappan 'Empire' seems to be less sustainable. In the first place, an empire envisages an emperor who, both in life and death, must distinguish himself from the rest. In other words, there ought to be 'palaces' on the one hand and 'royal tombs' on the other, such as we have in other contemporary civilizations. Unfortunately, in the case of the Harappan Civilization we have neither. Attempts have been made to identify some of the structures at Mohenjo-daro as palaces, but the case is far from satisfactory. And certainly there are no royal tombs. All the graves discovered so far, whether at Harappa or Kalibangan or Rakhigarhi or Lothal, are more or less of a modest order and none of them can lay claim to being that of an 'emperor'. Thus, the 'Empire' theory will have to remain in a 'suspense account', at least for the time being.

(VI) THE CHRONOLOGICAL HORIZON

John Marshall, in his report on the excavations at Mohenjo-daro, proposed a chronological horizon for the Indus/ Harappan Civilization on the basis of the occurrence of certain Harappan objects at various Mesopotamian sites, which had already been dated. Accordingly, he averred that 'the Indus Civilization must go back to an age before 2800 BC', and suggested an overall time-bracket of 3250-2750 BCE. Reviewing the position, in 1968, Mortimer Wheeler arrived at the following conclusion: 'it may now be postulated that the nuclear cities of the Indus Civilization were founded some time before 2400 BC, and they endured in same shape to eighteenth century BC, always with the reservation that these brackets cannot be expected to fit closely and mechanically to Indus towns and villages of all sizes and in all locations.' Then came an era for 'shorter chronology' and its exponents suggested an overall date of 2300-2000 BCE.

Finally came in the method of direct dating, namely that of radiocarbon. Though this method too has its own pitfalls, such as contamination of the samples with modern rootlets, successive changes in the half-life value and finally revisions of 'calibrations' themselves, it remains the best bid at present. I have discussed elsewhere (Lal 1997: 242-54) in great detail the C-14 dates from as many as seventeen different Harappan sites and the upshot is that the Mature stage of the Harappan Civilization ranged from ca. 2600 BCE to ca. 2000 BCE, with a possible, though limited, spill-over on the latter side.

CHAPTER FOUR

WHO WERE THESE HARAPPANS ? AN ENQUIRY INTO THEIR ETHNICITY

A. INTRODUCTORY

Ever since the discovery of the Harappan Civilization in the 1920s a debate has been going on about the authorship of this civilization. The excavator of Mohenjo-daro, John Marshall, held the view that the Dravidian-speaking people were the ones who created this civilization. This theory held sway for several decades. But in the course of time another view emerged, according to which it were the Vedic Aryans who were responsible for it. In the present chapter we propose to examine both these views and try to find out the truth. We would also examine the much-touted theory that there was an 'Aryan Invasion' of India as also a newly-hugged-to-the-chest thesis that if there was no 'Invasion', the Vedic people must have come as 'Immigrants' from the Bactria-Margiana region of Central Asia.

B. WHERE LIE THE SEEDS OF CONFUSION?

In the 19th century, the renowned German scholar Max Muller attempted to date the Vedas. Having no anchor, he chose to date them on a rather ad hoc basis. He accepted that the *Sūtra*s were in existence around the sixth century BCE. Before that were the stages to which belonged respectively the *Āraṇyaka*s, *Brāhmaṇa*s, and the *Veda*s themselves. He thought a period of 200 years would be good enough for each one of these stages. Thus, adding 600 years to the sixth century BCE, he arrived at 1,200 BCE as the date of the Vedas. On the principle that 'something is better than nothing', this dating may have given some bearing in the existing wilderness. However, the ad-hocism did not pass unnoticed. Thus, when Max Muller's contemporaries like Goldstucker, Whitney and Wilson seriously objected to this kind of approach, he relented and admitted (in his Preface to the *Ṛigveda*):

> I have repeatedly dwelt on the merely hypothetical character of the dates, which I have ventured to assign to the first periods of Vedic literature. All I have claimed for them has been that they are minimum dates, and that the literary productions of each period which either still exist or which formerly existed could hardly be accounted for within shorter limits of time than those suggested.

But this would not satisfy the critics. Max Muller then had to climb down, stating somewhat apologetically (1890, Reprint 1979):

> If now we ask how we can fix the dates of these periods, it is quite clear that we cannot hope to fix a *terminum a qua* [sic]. Whether the Vedic hymns were composed [in] 1000 or 1500 or 2000 or 3000 BC, no power on earth will ever determine.

However, the greatest irony is that in spite of such a candid surrender by Max Muller himself, his fatwa, once given, still rules the roost, at least in certain quarters, even though recent researches have proved that the Vedas are very much older than 1200 BCE, the date initially proposed by Max Muller.

Anyway, the fallout of the 1200-BCE-deadline soon became apparent. Thus, when the Harappan Civilization was discovered and dated to the third millennium BCE on the basis of the occurrence of certain artefacts of this civilization in the already-dated contexts in Mesopotamia, it seemed logical to deduce that since the Vedas were no older than 1200 BCE, as per Max Muller's fatwa, the Harappan Civilization could not be associated with the Vedic people. Further, since the only other major group in the country was that of the

Dravidian-speaking people, it was further argued that these very people were the authors of the Harappan Civilization.

C. WERE THE DRAVIDIAN-SPEAKING PEOPLE THE AUTHORS OF THE HARAPPAN CIVILIZATION?

The year 1946 saw yet another landmark in the historiography of the Harappan Civilization. As we shall discuss a little later in detail, in that year Mortimer Wheeler discovered a fortification wall at Harappa and taking a hint from the Vedas that Indra, the Aryan god, was a destroyer of forts (*puraṁdara*), he lost no time in declaring that the Harappan Civilization was destroyed by Aryan invaders. As a sequel to this invasion, came up another theory that the defeated Harappans were driven away all the way to South India, leaving only a small section behind. Further, in support of the residual Dravidian-speaking people is often cited the small section of the Brahui-speaking population in Baluchistan.

We shall first take up the Brahui issue. Most of the scholars who have studied this problem doubt if Brahui really belongs to the Dravidian group. Some of them even associate it with the eastern Elamite. Then there are scholars who hold that the Brahui-speaking people are not the original inhabitants of Baluchistan but migrated to that area during the mediaeval times. Thus, one really wonders how much weight can be given to the Brahui argument.

As to the thesis that the defeated Harappans were driven away to South India, the least said the better. If there was any truth in this premise, one would expect to find at least a few settlements of the displaced Harappans in South India. But the hard fact is that **nowhere in South India – whether it be in Tamil Nadu or Andhra Pradesh or Karnataka or Kerala – has even a single site associable with the Harappan Civilization been found.** On the other hand, what do we have in South India of that time is a neolithic culture, christened in Indian archaeology as the Southern Neolithic Culture. Are we then expected to believe that, on reaching South India, the Harappans overnight shed off their civilizational traits and took to a neolithic (Stone Age) way of life?

In this debate there is one more aspect which has to be taken note of. It has been noted all over the world that even when a new set of population takes over a given area and assigns new names in its own language to some towns and rivers, the pre-existing old names still continue to survive. As an example of this may be cited the case of the United States of America. When the Britishers and other Europeans ran over this territory they did no doubt gave new names to some of the townships and rivers, such as New Jersey, New York, Hudson, etc. but the old names in existence prior to the coming of these foreigners have survived: for example, Massachusetts and Chicago as place-names, or Mississippi and Missouri as names of rivers. Now, if there is any truth in the statement that the Harappans were a Dravidian-speaking people and that they were overrun by the Sanskrit-speaking Vedic people, one would expect a few Dravidian names of townships or rivers to have survived this supposed onslaught. But the hard fact is that there is not even a single Dravidian name in the one-time Harappan domain. Why? Simply because **the Harappans were not a Dravidian-speaking people.**

D. WAS THERE REALLY AN 'ARYAN INVASION'?

In the previous section there was a passing reference to the 'Aryan Invasion' syndrome. Here we shall examine the matter in detail.

To get back to Wheeler's excavations at Harappa in 1946. As stated earlier, he discovered a fortification wall around one of the mounds (Mound AB) at the site. This was something extremely new for the Harappan settlements, which were so far thought to have been unfortified. (Now, of course, we know that almost every metropolitan town of the Harappan Civilization was fortified. See Chapter III, Section B.) Anyway, an ex-Army Brigadier, Wheeler was so much excited about the discovery that he could not but interpret the fortifications only in terms of an invasion and defence. While he was still churning the whole issue in his mind, he learnt from a visiting scholar of repute that in the Vedas Indra had been referred to as a destroyer of forts (*puraṁdara*). And lo! Wheeler lost no time in declaring that there was an 'Aryan Invasion' which destroyed the

Harappan Civilization. Here is an excerpt from Wheeler's report on the excavations (1947: 82):

> The Aryan invasion of the Land of Seven Rivers, the Punjab and its environs, constantly assumes the form of an onslaught upon the walled cities of the aborigines. For these cities the term used in the *Ṛigveda* is *pur*, meaning a 'rampart', 'fort' or 'stronghold. ... Indra, the Āryan War-god, is *puraṁdara*, 'fort-destroyer'. He shatters 'ninety forts' for his Āryan protege Divodasa.
>
> Where are – or were – these citadels? It has in the past been supposed that they were mythical, or were 'merely places of refuge against attack, ramparts of hardened earth with palisades and a ditch'. The recent excavation at Harappa may be thought to have changed the picture. Here we have a slightly evolved civilization of essentially non-Āryan type, now known to have employed massive fortifications, and known also to have dominated the river-system of northwestern India at a time not distant from the likely period of the earlier Āryan invasions of the region. What destroyed this firmly settled civilization? Climatic, economic, political deterioration may have weakened it, but its ultimate **extinction** is more likely to have been completed by deliberate and large-scale destruction. It may be no mere chance that at a late period of Mohenjo-daro men, women and children appear to have been massacred there. **On circumstantial evidence, Indra stands accused.**

The 'Aryan Invasion' theory, so categorically enunciated by Wheeler, has many a flaw. Besides banking on the existence of a fortification wall at Harappa and the portrayal of Indra as *puraṁdara* in the Vedas, Wheeler no less heavily leans on the presence of some skeletal remains at Mohenjo-daro, which he holds were those of the people massacred by the invading Aryans. Now, if there is any truth in the allegation that this was the result of a massacre, one expects that all these skeletons would have come from one and the same stratum, in fact from the latest stratum after which the site would have been abandoned. But this is **not** the case. During the nine years of excavation at this site a total of thirty-seven skeletons were found, some complete and others fragmentary. And these came from different levels – some from the Intermediate level, some from the Late level and still some others from the debris which had accumulated after the desertion of the site. How then can these be attributed to a single event, namely that of invasion and a massacre resulting therefrom? Secondly, some of the skeletons bore cut-marks which had been healed. One knows that cut-marks take time to heal. If the death in these cases had occurred as a result of a war-massacre, it would have been instantaneous and there would have been no time for any kind of healing. Thirdly, all the skeletons came from the Lower Town alone, which was inhabited by the common folks, and not from the Citadel wherein dwelt those who commanded the settlement. Does it not look strange that the (supposed) invaders deemed it necessary to attack and kill the commoners only, carefully sparing the 'rulers' or elites? And finally, if it was an invasion, **one expects the invaders to have left at the site some vestiges,** by way of their arms or some others equipment. **Nothing of the kind was found.** Indeed, George F. Dales (1964) was perfectly justified in castigating it as a **'mythical massacre'.**

Furthermore, if there was even the slightest truth in the theory of 'Aryan Invasion' and the 'extinction' of the Harappan Civilization as set forth by Wheeler, one would expect at least some of the other Harappan sites to corroborate the (misconstrued) Mohenjo-daro evidence. But the hard fact is that **no other site has yielded any such evidence**, be it Amri or Kot Diji, located not far away from Mohenjo-daro, or Harappa itself in the neighbouring Punjab or Kalibangan in Rajasthan or Banawali and Rakhigarhi in Haryana or Lothal, Surkotada and Dholavira in Gujarat. **Nor have any material remains of an alien culture been found at any of these site. Indeed, in the entire area covered by the Harappan Civilization nowhere do have either the vestiges of any wanton destruction or the presence of any alien culture. Whether the protagonists of the 'Aryan Invasion' theory like it not, 'Indra' no longer 'stands accused'. Indeed, he stands** ***exonerated!***

Dales and I are not the only ones who thoroughly discount the 'Aryan Invasion' theory. There are many others too. For example, commenting on Wheeler's theory, a distinguished archaeologist from his own country, Colin Renfrew (1988: 188 and 190), observed:

> When Wheeler speaks of 'the Aryan invasion of the Land of Seven Rivers, the Punjab', he has no warranty at all, so far as I can see. If one checks the dozen reference in the Rig Veda to the seven rivers, **there is nothing in any of them that to me implies an invasion. ... Despite Wheeler's comments, it is difficult to see what is particularly non-Aryan about the Indus valley.**

And here are Jim G. Shaffer and Diane Lichtenstein (1999), from across the Atlantic, who smell a rat in such allegations as the 'Aryan Invasion'.

> A few scholars have proposed that there is nothing in the 'literature' firmly placing the Indo-Aryans outside of South Asia, and **now archaeological record is confirming this.** ... As data accumulate to support cultural continuity in South Asian prehistoric and historic periods, a considerable restructuring of existing interpretive paradigms must take place. **We reject most strongly the simplistic historical interpretations, which date back to the eighteenth century, that continue to be imposed on south Asian cultural history. These still prevailing interpretations are significantly diminished by European ethnocentrism, colonialism, racism and antisemitism.**

E. AN ATTEMPT AT BACKDOOR ENTRY

The deeply ingrained belief that the Vedic people must have come to India from outside has led many a scholar to seek other kinds of approach. Thus, the renowned scholar, Gregory L. Possehl writes (1996:65): 'One thing seems certain; the speakers of Vedic Sanskrit ... came from elsewhere. This conclusion comes from ... Indo-European words for trees which are species such as birch, Scotch pine, linden, alder and oak. These are plants from a temperate environment and the fact that their names are shared among the early languages of the family suggests a homeland in this environment.'

The evidence of Ṛigvedic flora and fauna has been dealt with at great length in one of my books (2005) and it is not proposed to repeat all that here. In summary, however, let it be squarely stated that the *Ṛigveda*, the earliest book of the Aryans, does **not** mention any of the species of cold-climate trees enumerated above by Possehl. On the other hand, **all the trees mentioned in the *Ṛigveda*, such as the *Aśvattha***

(***Ficus religosa* L.), *Khadira* (*Acacia catechu* Willd.), *Nyagrodha* (*Ficus benghalensis* L.,** Pl. XXIII**), *Vibhidaka* (*Terminalia bellerica* Roxb.) to name just a few, do not belong to a cold climate but to a tropical one.** Likewise, the **Ṛigvedic fauna,** comprising such species as the lion, elephant, peacock (Pl. XXIV), **also belongs to a tropical climate and does not include any species specific to cold climate.**

It is thus abundantly clear that the Vedic Aryans cannot be pushed in even through a back door, taking refuge under a cold-climate fauna.

F. IF THERE WAS NO 'ARYAN INVASION', WAS THERE AN 'ARYAN IMMIGRATION'?

(I) CLAIMS OF ROMILA THAPAR AND R.S. SHARMA

While writing this Section, I am reminded of Oliver Goldsmith's poem, *The Village School Master.* In it, the poet refers to a characteristic habit of the School Master, which, in the poets own words, was: 'Even though vanquished, he would argue still!'

Finding that the 'Aryan Invasion' theory has no archaeological basis whatsoever, some of those who had once sworn by it have now come out with a new 'green channel' to let in the Aryans from outside. Thus, Professor Romila Thapar (1989-91: 259-60) spins out the hypothesis: 'If invasion is discarded then the mechanism of migration and occasional contacts come into sharper focus. The migrations appear to have been of **pastoral cattle breeders** who are prominent in the *Āvestā* and *Ṛigveda*,'

A close compeer of Thapar, Professor R.S. Sharma, amplifies this concept. Says he (1999: 77): '... The pastoralists who moved to the Indian borderland came from Bactria-Margiana Archaeological Complex or BMAC which saw the genesis of the culture of the *Ṛigveda.*'

Evidently, both Thapar and Sharma are still under the spell of the 19th century paradigms according to which (i) the Aryans were nomads and (ii) they must have come from outside. But have these learned scholars even once had a look at the cultural components of the Bactria-Margiana Archaeological Complex (BMAC)? Perhaps not. Had they cared to do so, they would have straightaway realized that the **authors of the BMAC are *not* 'pastoral cattle breeders'.** As would be shown in the following few pages, **they had all the trappings of urbanism**, be it town-planning (including well laid-out temples and palaces), excellent metal industries, superb works of art in limestone, chlorite and gold, intricately carved seals, and so on. Further, none of the characteristic features of the BMAC ever entered the territory east of the Indus (see maps at Figs. 4.9 and 4.10). Thus, it was high time that these two scholars, and their ilk, withdrew their plans to 'smuggle' the BMAC people into India.

(II) Some Characteristic Features of the BMAC

I am sure by now the reader would be keen to know what after all the BMAC really is. Several eminent archaeologists, like Victor I. Sarianidi, have carried out in recent decades extensive excavations at a number of sites in the area extending from Margiana in Turkmenistan on the west to Bactria in northern Afghanistan on the east (Fig. 4.1) and have brought to light an urban civilization which now goes by the name of Bactria-Margiana Archaeological Complex. In its Mature Stage, it is datable to circa 2000-1700 BCE. We

Fig. 4.1. Region of Bactria-Margiana Archaeological Complex.

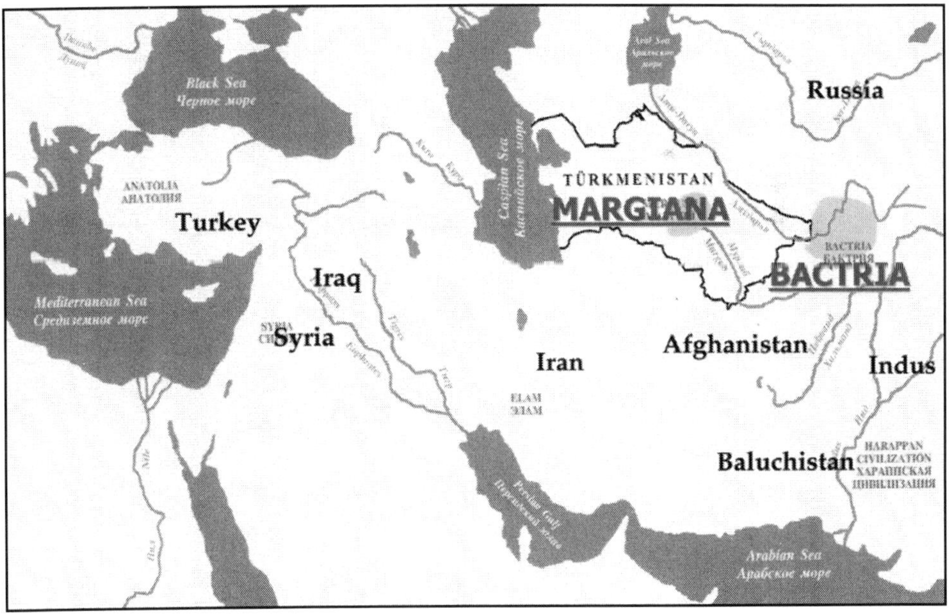

shall not go into very many details over here, but enough to demonstrate the high calibre of this civilization – which, in its own right, claims a seat along with the ancient civilizations of Egypt, Iraq, Iran, India and China.

(a) Town-Planning and Monumental Architecture

Here we draw attention to only two complexes, one secular and the other religious. At Gonur, in Margiana, has been discovered a 'Citadel' or a 'Kremlin', the latter name having been given evidently after the famous Kremlin in Moscow, the centre of governmental activities. The Gonur Kremlin, covering an area of 115 x 120 metres, was enclosed by a fortification wall which was reinforced with a rectangular tower at each corner and four rectangular towers on each side. Within it were located the king's residence, halls for official functions, an administrative block and an area earmarked even for burial rites (Pl. XXV).

The temple-complex at Togolok-21 is, again, an elaborate affair. Covering an overall area of 1.5 hectares, the complex has a series of three successive enclosure walls. Of these, the innermost wall, having a thickness of 5 metres, surrounds an area 60 x 50 metres and has one circular tower at each corner and one semi-circular tower at the middle of the eastern and western sides. Following more or less the same pattern, there are two more successive walls on the exterior. Fig. 4.2 gives not only a plan of the complex but also an isometric projection thereof.

(b) Metal Axes

From the BMAC graves as well as from the habitation deposits various metal objects have been recovered. These are mostly of copper/bronze, but sometimes of silver and gold too. Of these, we illustrate here only the axes. Two of these, made of copper, have respectively a seated human figure and an animal at the butt-end (Pl. XXVI). The third, however, is remarkable in many ways (Pl. XXVII). First, it is made of silver and is covered with a gold lamina. Secondly, at the butt-end there are a winged feline and heads of two eagles, while on the body too some figures have been depicted: all this may probably be having some mythological bearing. Anyway, it is evident that this highly decorated, silver/gold axe was not meant for cutting firewood or for

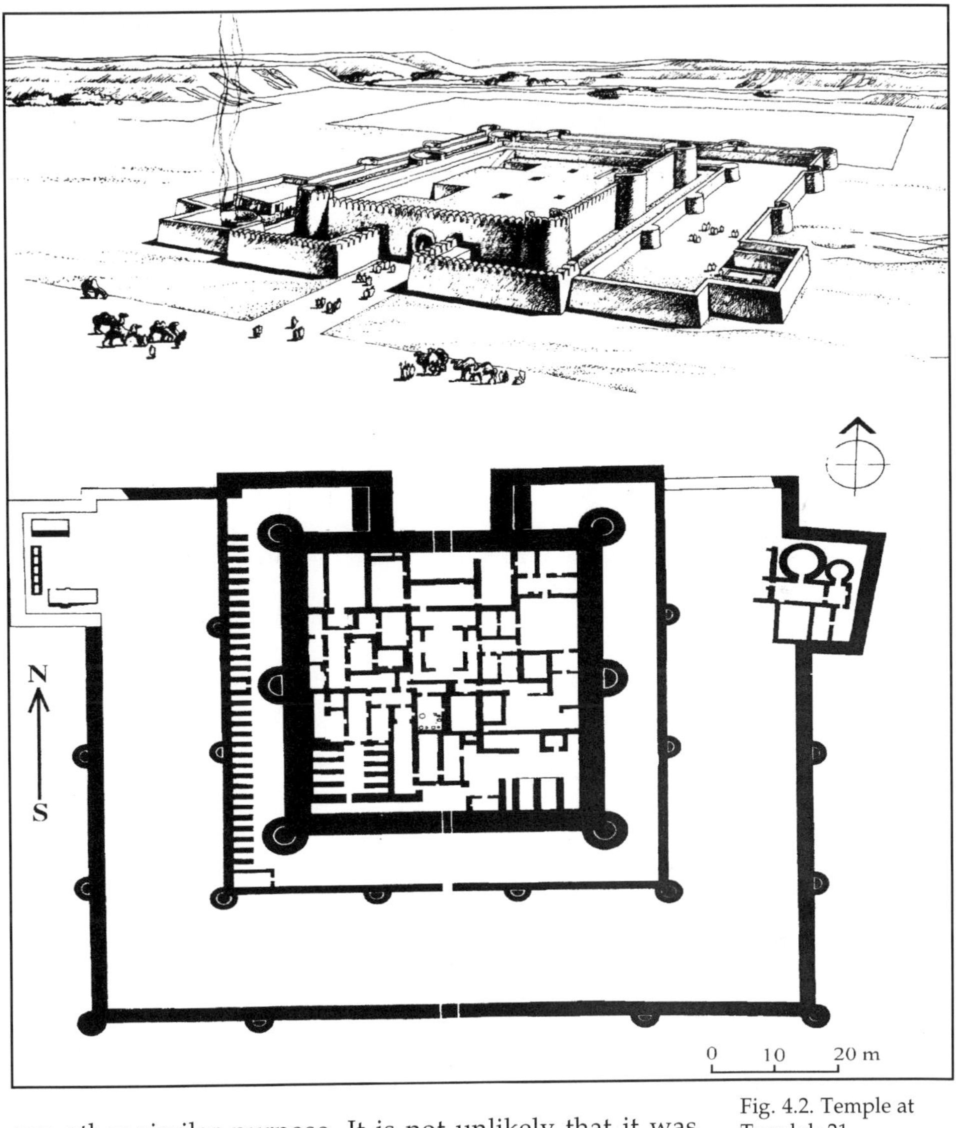

Fig. 4.2. Temple at Togolok-21, Margiana.

any other similar purpose. It is not unlikely that it was mounted on a specially prepared staff which was held by a ruler/king as the symbol of authority.

(c) Some Cult Objects

Amongst the various cult objects there are two types which call for special attention. In one category are earthen bowls

Left: Fig. 4.3. Togolok-1, Margiana: A Cult vessel (pottery) from the temple.

Right: Fig. 4.4. Togolok-21, Margiana: 'Dainty columns' of stone from the temple.

having a freeze of small animals (sometimes humans as well) running along the rim. Besides, there are serpents crawling up and down along the interior and exterior walls (Fig. 4.3). Because of the presence of animal and human figures along the rim, these bowls are clearly not meant for ordinary use, as drinking bowls. Hence the possibility of their having been associated with some kind of ritual. In the other category come what are known as 'diminutive' or 'dainty' columns (Fig. 4.4). Made of multi-coloured stone, these are about half-metre in height, well polished and usually have a groove.

(d) Sculptural Art

Carved out of stone, the sculptures include both human and animal figures. All these throw very valuable light on the artistic acumen of the BMAC people. For example, on Pl. XXVIII is shown a female figure, to depict which the sculptor has used a pinkish stone for the face and hands, but a blackish one for the dress which is not monotonous but brings out a pleasing herring-bone weave.

And no less remarkable – or perhaps more – is a feline made of chlorite stone (Pl. XXX). But the sculptor did not end up with the stone. He has given a covering of gold leaf which in turn is punctuated with a variety of semi-precious stones. Isn't it breath-taking? Attention may also be drawn to a limestone goat whose horns, eyes and beard are shown in lapis lazuli (Pl. XXIX).

(e) Amulets and Seals

Equally interesting are the amulets and seals which throw

valuable light on the religious concepts and mythologies of the BMAC people. Made of black steatite, the amulets depict a variety of motifs among which particular attention is drawn by such items as scorpions, snakes, eagles, felines and the typical two-humped Bactrian camel. The seals, made usually of copper/bronze but sometimes of silver as well, bear, besides some of the foregoing motifs, geometric designs as well. But the most remarkable and intriguing are the cylinder seals which narrate what look like mythological scenes. (Some of the latter will be dealt with in detail a little later.)

(iii) Sarianidi's Claim

While giving accolades to this eminent archaeologist for his untiring efforts to place the BMAC on an international footing, we do have reservations about his interpretation of the data when he calls the BMAC people as the forebears of the Iranian and Indo-Aryans. In July 2007 I delivered an Inaugural Address, captioned 'Let not the 19th Century Paradigms continue to haunt us!', at the 19th International Conference on South Asian Archaeology, held at the University of Bologna, Ravenna (Lal 2007; it is also under publication in the Proceedings of the Conference.) In it I discussed at some length this untenable claim of Professor Sarianidi. But here I will go only briefly into the matter, since I do not want the reader of this book to be overburdened with details.

The main pillars on which Sarianidi erects his edifice are: (i) fire-worship temples of the BMAC; (ii) supposed use of the *soma/haoma* in the BMAC rituals; (iii) (mistaken) *aśvamedha* sacrifice; and (iv) cult motifs on the BMAC seals. We shall briefly deal with all these four aspects.

(a) Fire Worship

We begin with a quotation from Sarianidi himself (1933a: 679): 'A building unearthed at Gonur *temenos* and conveniently called a fort has a cross-shaped general plan with twelve corner towers. It most closely resembles the outer contours of the indisputable fire temple at Tepe Nush-i-Jan. A difference of minor importance only consists of the fact that while the towers are round at Gonur, they are square at Nush-i-Jan'. While a general comparison between the outer

Fig. 4.5. Fort at Gonur and Temple at Nush-i-Jan.

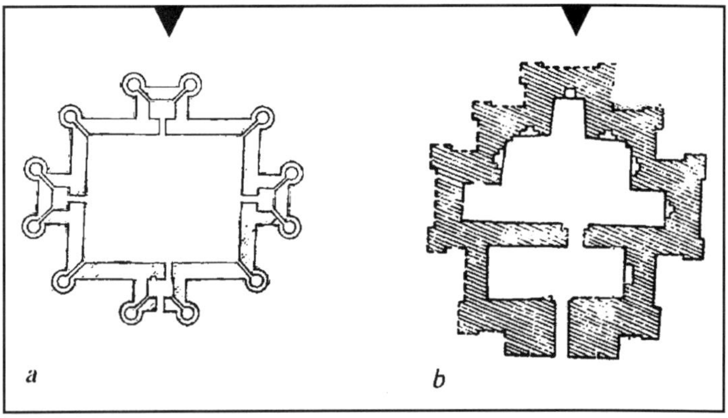

plans of the two structures (Fig. 4.5) may be all right to some extent, the weakness lies in the fact that the plan of the interior of the *temenos* at Gonur is **not** at all clear, as admitted by Sarianidi himself: 'Unfortunately, the fort (at Gonur temenos) appears to be **unfinished** so we do not know its inner construction, but apparently it was a fire temple.' This 'apparentness' would not do, since in such crucial matters what is needed is solid evidence to prove that the Gonur *temenos* really was a fire temple.

Anyway, leaving it to specialists in Zoroastrian religion and architecture to accept or reject the claim of Sarianidi in respect of the Gonur *temenos* as being a Zoroastrian fire temple, I would certainly like to offer my comments on his claim that a structural complex at Mohenjo-daro was a fire temple. On p. 676 of the paper cited above Sarianidi states: 'An example is the fire temple in the lower town of Mohenjo-daro; its basic plan comprises a courtyard encompassed by corridors (Dhavalikar and Atre 1989)'.

Sarianidi has chosen to jump into the wand wagon of Dhavalikar and Atre who themselves have indulged in a series of conjectures – ifs and buts – to imagine that this structure (Fig. 4.6) was a fire temple. **The excavator of Mohenjo-daro, John Marshall, very categorically takes it to have been a residential house** (Marshall 1931, Vol. I: 202). More important, in his anxiety to rope in India as well in a Zoroastrian kind of fire worship, Sarianidi has completely lost sight of the trap into which he has fallen. **Did he ever realize that the Mohenjo-daro structure belongs to the third**

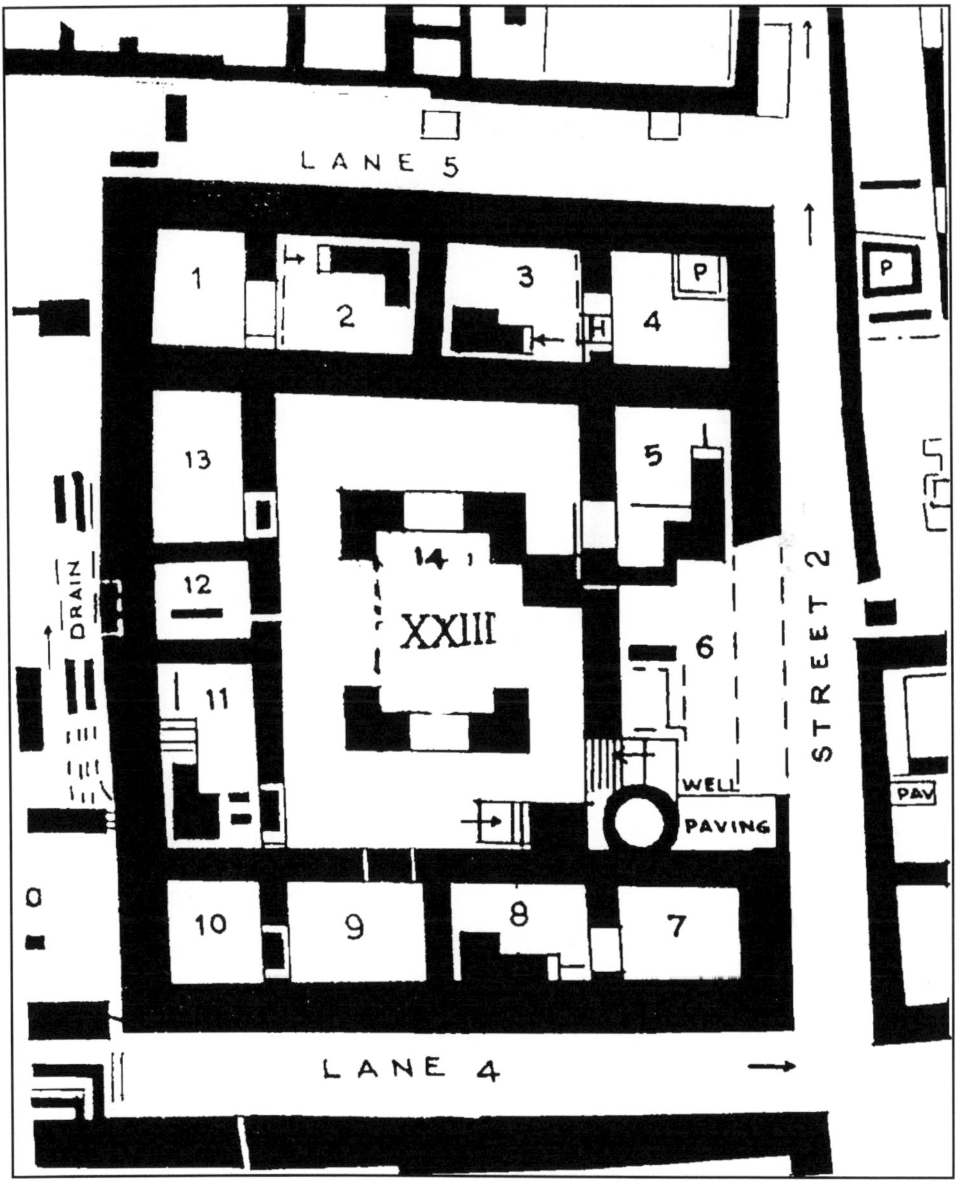

Fig. 4.6. Mohenjo-daro: 'Fire Temple'?

millennium BCE whereas the BMAC is a second-millennium BCE phenomenon? If he does stick to his stand, he will have to concede that Zoroastrianism originated in India and thence travelled to BMAC. Is he a game for this?

(b) The Soma/Haoma

The *soma* was a sacred drink during the Ṛigvedic times. The same drink, going by the name of *Haoma* (the sibilant '*s*' changing into '*h*'), has been referred to in the *Āvestā*. Sarianidi claims that its remains have been found in the BMAC temples. The actual substances found are reported to be hemp, poppy and ephedra. In modern Indian terminology the intoxicating substances derived from these plants are respectively *gāñjā, afīma* and *bhāṅga*. I am not very sure if the first two can really lay claim to being the *soma/haoma* of the ancient texts, since *gāñjā* is smoked and *afīma* is eaten, whereas the *soma* was drunk according to the Vedic texts. It is only *bhāṅga* (ephedra) that is drunk. But not many scholars are inclined to accept even the ephedra as being ancient *soma/haoma*. Anyway, we give below an extract from a report by Harri Nyberg, an acknowledged authority on the subject (1995: 400):

> ... remains of ephedras have also been reported from the temple-fortress complex of Togolok 21 in the Merv oasis (ancient Margiana – Parpola 1988; Meier-Melikyan 1990) along with the remains of poppies. ... In 1990 I received some samples from the site [forwarded by Dr. Fred Hiebert of Harvard University], which were subjected to pollen analysis at the Department of Botany, University of Helsinki. ... The largest amount of pollen was found in the bone tube (used for imbibing liquid?) from Gonur 1, but even in this sample, which had been preserved in a comparatively sheltered position when compared with the other investigated samples, **only pollen of the family Caryophyllaceae was present.** ***No pollen from ephedras or poppies was found*** and even the pollen left in the samples showed clear traces of deterioration (typical in ancient pollen having been preserved in a dry environment in contact with oxygen). **Our pollen analysis was carefully checked for any methodological errors, but no inaccuracies were found.**

When the very evidence is so much shaky, how can we make far-reaching conclusions that the BMAC people are ancestral to the Zoroastrians of Iran and the Vedic people of India?

(c) The Aśvamedha

Although Professor Sarianidi has been publishing off and on the skeletal remains of the horse from his excavations in Margiana, he has given a useful summary of these findings in a paper recently presented at a conference, of which he has very kindly sent me a copy. (However, the date and place of the conference are not mentioned in that paper.) I am basing my discussion on what is mentioned in this paper.

Altogether 'remains of six horses have been found at the North Gonur capital site in Margiana'. One of these pertains to a 'young horse buried inside a mausoleum of mud bricks'. Then there is a 'foal burial at the territory of the Gonur royal necropolis'. 'Remains of three other domestic horses have been found in the elite tombs'. The sixth skeleton is that of a 'young horse, without a head and a tail, found at necropolis'. Adds Sarianidi: '[It] **unintentionally reminds of the ancient Indian ritual *aśvamedha*.**' This, he holds, is an additional evidence, besides that of *soma* already mentioned, of the BMAC people having been the ancestors of the Vedic Aryans.

While the first five skeletons do not call for any comments, it is the last one that does. In an earlier publication, Sarianidi had also published a photograph of it and I take the opportunity of reproducing the same here (Pl. XXXI). It would be noticed that there is no outline of the pit, if there ever was one, in which the horse is supposed to have been given a burial. Secondly, the skeleton lies hardly a few centimetres below the ground-level, seen at top-left. All this would imply that it is not a case of regular burial of the horse. The absence of the head of the horse, which has led Sarianidi to believe that it was a case of horse-sacrifice (*aśvamedha*), may as well be due to a variety of other reasons, such as erosion through natural agencies or even subsequent human vandalism.

In addition to the foregoing, the most important point is that the skeletal remains do not conform to what is laid down in the Vedic texts in respect of the *aśvamedha*. The *Ṛigveda* contains two *Sūkta*s exclusively devoted to the *aśvamedha*, viz. 1.162 and 1.163. Interested readers may go through these, but I quote here just one hymn (1.162.18) to give an idea. It runs as follows:

> The four-and-thirty ribs of the swift Charger, kin to the Gods, the slayer's hatchet pierces.
> Cut ye with skill, so that the parts be flawless, and piece by piece declaring them **dissect them**. (Griffith's translation of the *Ṛigveda*, Vol. I, p. 216)

It would thus be seen that in the *aśvamedha* sacrifice the horse had to be dissected piece by piece, whereas in the case of the Gonur horse, taken by Sarianidi to represent an *aśvamedha*, there is no such evidence whatsoever. Must not Sarianidi re-think before insisting on this as an evidence of the BMAC people being the ancestors of the Ṛigvedic Aryans?

(d) Motifs on BMAC Glyptics

Lastly, Sarianidi draws heavily on the motifs on the BMAC seals as a proof the BMAC people having been the ancestors of the Indo-Aryans. Perhaps the best course would be to quote from the writings of Sarianidi himself (1993b: 12-13):

> In this connection worthy of utmost attention is the impression of a cylinder seal on one of the Margianian vessels, found... at Gonur. The central figure of a frequently repeated frieze composition is a standing nude anthropomorphic winged deity with an avian head holding two mountain goats by the legs...
>
> Such anthropomorphic winged and avian-headed deities are represented fairly fully in the glyptics and on the seals of Bactria. ... These Bactrian images find the most impressive correspondence in Syro-Hittite glyptics.
>
> If the fact that it's for the Mitanni kingdom that the names of Aryan deities are evidenced is taken into account the importance of the Bactrian-Margianian images will become obvious in the light of solving the Aryan problem on the basis of new archaeological data.

To put it simply, Sarianidi's logic is like this. Certain motifs on the BMAC seals compare well with those on the Syro-Hittite glyptics. Hence there is a cultural relationship between the two areas. Further, since a Hittite-Mitanni treaty (the Bogazkoy one) refers to the Vedic gods like Indra, Mitra, Varuṇa, etc., there is a strong case (according to him) for the BMAC people being ancestral to the Vedic Aryans.

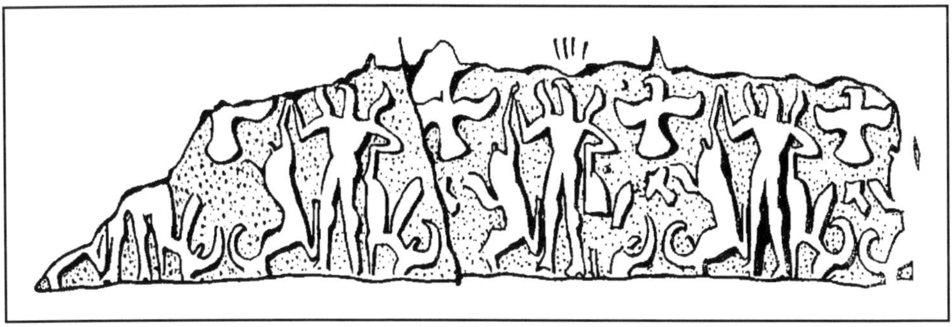

Fig. 4.7. Impression of cylinder seal from Gonur-1.

In the above quotation from Sarianidi there is a specific reference to a seal which depicts 'a standing nude anthropomorphic winged deity with an avian head, holding two mountain goats by the legs (here Fig. 4.7). May not one ask Sarianidi: 'Which Aryan god does he see in this anthropomorphic figure? Indra, Mitra, Varuṇa or Nāsatya? Or does the narrative correspond to any Vedic story?'

There is yet another seal published by Sarianidi, which I would like to place before the reader (Fig. 4.8). It shows two figures with human body and animal head, holding a tall wooden (?) pillar on the pointed top of which rests the belly of another animal-headed human being. The scene further depicts a few more similar figures playing on drum, etc. One really wonders which Vedic myth does Sarianidi see in this narrative?

Fig. 4.8. Cylinder seal from Togolok-21 and its impression.

Besides these intrinsic flaws in Sarianidi's BMAC ancestry of the Vedic Aryans, there is a much greater

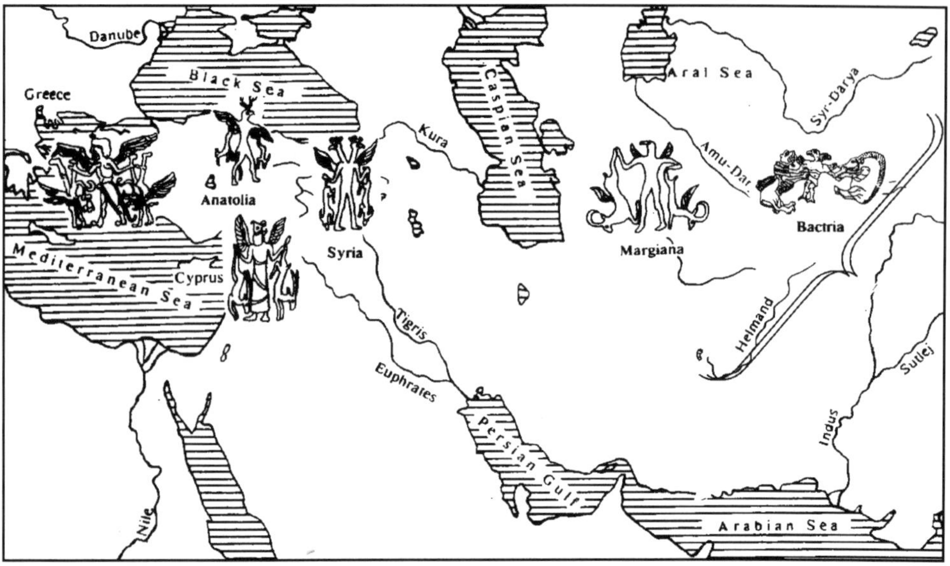

Fig. 4.9. Spread of the motif of man-bird with hit animals.

weakness in his thesis. In this context, I would like to draw the reader's attention to two maps (Figs. 4.9 and 4.10) published by Sarianidi himself (in 1993b: Figs. 2 and 5 respectively). Of these, the former shows the distribution of the avian-headed deity holding mountain goats. The occurrence is from the BMAC region on the east to the Syro-Hittite region on the west. There is no occurrence of it in southern Afghanistan or Baluchistan. The other map shows the distribution of 'diminutive columns' and 'ritual bowls'. It would be seen that in this case the provenance does go a bit southwards, into the region of Baluchistan. **But altogether, none of the aforesaid motifs or objects ever cross the Indus, entering the region occupied by the Vedic Aryans, as clearly specified in the Ṛigvedic hymns 10. 75. 5-6 (see pp. 115 and 126). Then where is a case for the supposed BMAC immigration into Vedic India?**

Here it would be unfair not to bring into the discussion some seals/seal-impressions from Gilund and Chanhu-daro which have a resemblance to certain seals from the BMAC region (Possehl 2004). Also may be brought into the picture an animal-headed antimony rod of copper from Harappa (Vats 1940, reprint 1974, pl. CXXV, 36) and a spiral-headed copper pin from Chanhu-daro (Mackay 1943, reprint 1976,

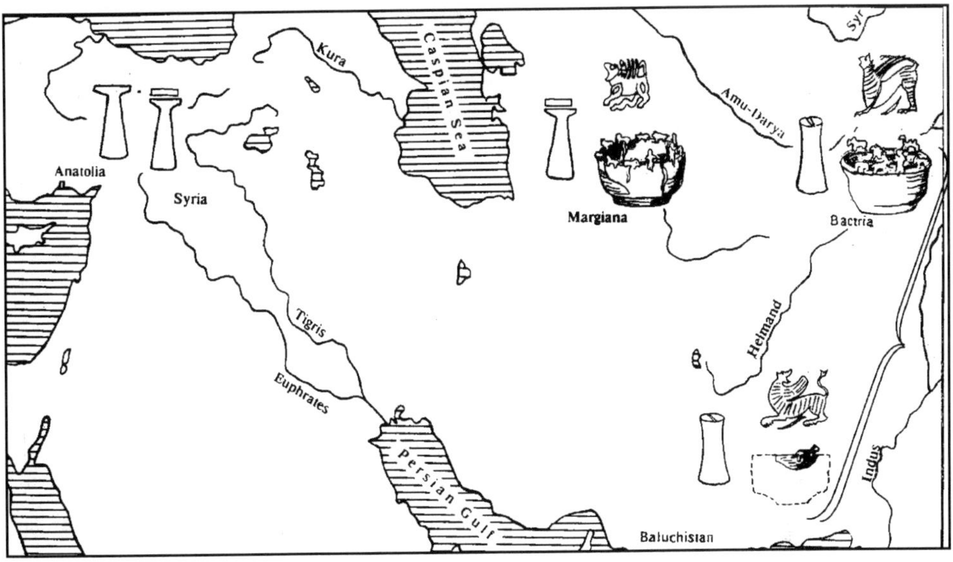

Fig. 4.10. Spread of 'diminutive columns' and their probable prototype in the Syro-Hittite world.

pl. LXVIII, 9), which are similar to those from the BMAC. But these two latter objects belong to the Harappan Civilization and are chronologically earlier than the BMAC. Anyway, the occurrence of a few odd objects east of the Indus cannot be construed to signify 'immigration' of BMAC people into India. Have we not in the past attributed the presence of a number of characteristic Harappan objects, such as etched carnelian beads, seals, etc. in West Asia, Iran and Central Asia, to trade and similar other mechanisms rather than an 'emigration' of the Harappan population into these regions? Then why invoke 'immigration' of the BMAC people in the case of the few objects referred to at the beginning of this paragraph?

G. EVIDENCE OF HUMAN BIOLOGY AND DNA

While concluding this Section on the supposed 'immigration' of the Vedic people from central Asia, I would like to draw the reader's pointed attention to the following evidence of two quite independent sciences, namely human biology and DNA.

After a detailed study of a large number of human skeletons from various ancient sites in India, B.E. Hemphill and his colleagues arrived at the following conclusion (1991:

137): 'As for the question of biological continuity within the Indus Valley, two discontinuities appear to exist. The first occurs between 6000 and 4500 BC. ... The second occurs at some point after 800 BC but before 200 BC.' It is, therefore, absolutely clear that **there was no immigration of any alien people between 4500 and 800 BCE.** Where then is the evidence of an 'invasion' by or even 'immigration' of the Vedic people, which some scholars think took place around 1500 BCE?

Further. In recent years a great deal of genetic research has been carried out which throws valuable light on this specific issue and I quote here Sanghamitra Sahoo et al. (2006: 843-48): 'The sharing of some Y-chromosomal haplogroups between Indian and Central Asian populations is most parsimoniously explained by a deep, common ancestry between the two regions, **with the diffusion of some Indian-specific lineages northward. The Y-chromosomal data consistently suggest a largely South Asian origin for Indian caste communities and therefore argue against any major influx, from regions north and west of India, of people associated either with the development of agriculture or the spread of the Indo-Aryan language family.**'

What more do we want?

H. THE CHRONOLOGICAL HORIZON OF THE *ṚIGVEDA*

As mentioned earlier, Max Muller's dating of the *Ṛigveda* to 1200 BCE was at the root of the entire confusion relating to the ethnic identity of the authors of the Harappan Civilization. It is, therefore, imperative to examine the dating afresh.

The mention of a shift of vernal equinox from Mṛigaśiras to Rohiṇī in the *Aitareya Brāhmaṇa* has led many astronomers to assign this text to ca. 3500 BCE and thus the Vedas to the 4th millennium BCE. Likewise, on the basis of the linguistic data, many other scholars (e.g. Kazanas 2001) also place the *Ṛigveda* in the 4th millennium BCE. Not being either an astronomer or a linguist, I am not in a position to offer any worthwhile comments. At the same time, I feel that these datings do call for attention. The best course, to my mind, would be to organize international seminars and try to thrash out these issues.

I would, however, now like to pass on to some down-to-earth evidence from a variety of sciences such as archaeology, hydrology, geology, radiocarbon-dating, etc. In this context, the history of the Ṛigvedic river Sarasvatī plays a very vital role. Unfortunately, however, some scholars have made the initial mistake of identifying it with the Helmand of Afghanistan (Sharma 1999: 35 and Habibs 1991-92). This is totally wrong.

If we are looking for the of Ṛigvedic Sarasvatī, we must look into the *Ṛigveda* itself and find out what it has to say in the matter. In it there is a very famous hymn, sung as a prayer to the rivers, viz. 10.75, whose Verses 5 and 6 mention the rivers known to the Ṛigvedic people, in a serial order from the Gaṅgā on the east to the Indus and its tributaries on the west. It runs as follows:

> *imam me* ***Gaṅge Yamune Sarasvati Śutudri*** *stomam sachatā Paruṣṇyā /*
> *Asiknyā Marudvṛidhe Vitastyā Ārjīkīye śṛiṇuhyā Suṣomayā //5//*
> *Tṛiṣṭāmayā prathamam yātave sajūḥ Susartvā Rasayā Śvetyā tyā /*
> *tvam Sindho Kubhayā Gomatīm Krumum Mehatnvā saratham yābhirīyase //6//*

> O Gaṅgā, Yamunā, Sarasvatī, Śutudrī (Sutlej) and Paruṣṇī (Ravi), O Marudvṛidhā with Asiknī (Chenab), O Ārjikīyā with Vitastā (Jhelum) and Suṣomā (Sohan), please listen to and accept this hymn of mine. [5]

> O Sindhu (Indus), flowing, you first meet the Tṛiṣṭāmā (and then) the Susartu, the Rasā, and the Śvetā (Swat), and thereafter the Kubhā (Kabul), the Gomatī (Gomal), the Krumu (Kurram) with the Mehatnu; and (finally) you move on in the same chariot with them (i.e. carry their waters with you). [6]

From these verses it is abundantly clear that the Sarasvatī lay between the Yamunā and Sutlej. Then, *RV* 3.23.4 states that the Dṛiṣadvatī and Āpayā were its tributaries (*Dṛiṣadvatyām mānuṣa Āpayām Sarasvatyām revadagne didīhi* ...). Further, *RV* 7.95.2 mentions that the Sarasvatī flowed all the way from the mountains to the sea (*ekāchetat Sarasvatī nadīnām śuchir yatī giribhya ā samudrāt* ...). In Afghanistan there are no rivers by the name of Yamunā and Sutlej, nor are there the Dṛiṣadvatī and Āpayā. Further, there is no sea in Afghanistan. So how can the Ṛigvedic Sarasvatī be placed there? **All this evidence – negative in the case of**

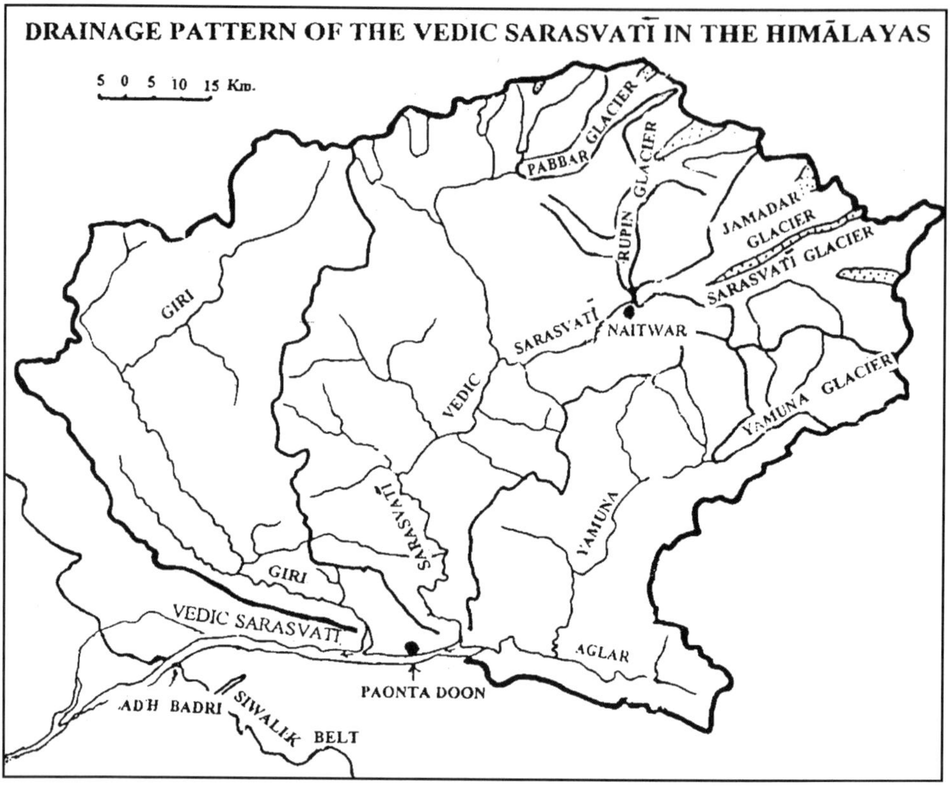

Fig. 4.11. Drainage Pattern of the Vedic Sarasvatī in the Himalayas.

Afghanistan but positive in the case of India – clinches the issue: the present-day Sarasvatī-Ghaggar combine, though now dry at places, does represent the Ṛigvedic Sarasvatī Fig. 4.11 shows its source in the Himalayas, Fig. 4.12 records its course on the plains of Haryana, Rajasthan and Cholistan (Pakistan), while Fig. 4.13 shows its final journey to the sea.

There is yet another piece of literary evidence that needs to be cited. Whereas during the Ṛigvedic times the Sarasvatī was a mighty flowing river, by the time of the *Pañchaviṁśa Brāhmaṇa* (XXV.10.16) it got dried up. Thus, on literary grounds, the *Ṛigveda* is to be dated prior to the drying up of the Sarasvatī, while the *Pañchaviṁśa Brāhmaṇa* would be posterior to that event.

Now to the archaeological evidence. Located on the bank of this ancient Sarasvatī (now called the Ghaggar) was the

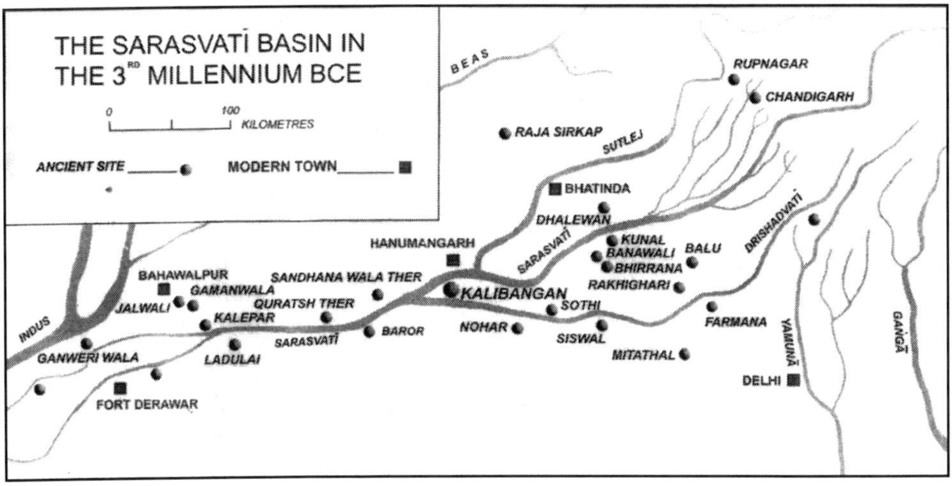

Fig. 4.12. The Sarasvatī Basin in the 3rd millennium BCE.

well known Harappan settlement of Kalibangan in Rajasthan. It had to be abandoned, while it was still in a mature stage, because of the drying up of the adjacent Sarasvatī river. This evidence has been thoroughly worked out by a team of Italian and Indian hydrologists, and Raikes, the leader, aptly captions his paper (1968): 'Kalibangan: Death from Natural Causes.' According to the radiocarbon dates, this abandonment took place around 2000-1900 BCE (Lal 1997: 245). Eminent geologists, V.M.K. Puri and B.C. Verma (1998), have demonstrated how the Sarasvatī originated from the Himalayan glaciers (Fig. 4.11) and how subsequently its channel got blocked because of tectonic movements in the Himalayas, which gave rise to the Bata-Markanda Divide (Fig. 4.14). As a result, the original channel dried up and its water got diverted to the Yamunā.

Putting together the entire archaeological, radiocarbon-dating, hydrological, geological and literary evidence, the following conclusion becomes inescapable, viz. that **since during the Ṛigvedic times the Sarasvatī was a mighty flowing river and according to the archaeological-radiocarbon-dating-cum-hydrological evidence this river dried up around 2000 BC, the *Ṛigveda* has got to be earlier than 2000 BC. How much earlier, it would, of course, be anybody's guess. In any case, at least a 3rd-millennium BCE horizon is indicated.**

Fig. 4.13. Lower Sindh and Kachchh in the 3rd millennium BC.

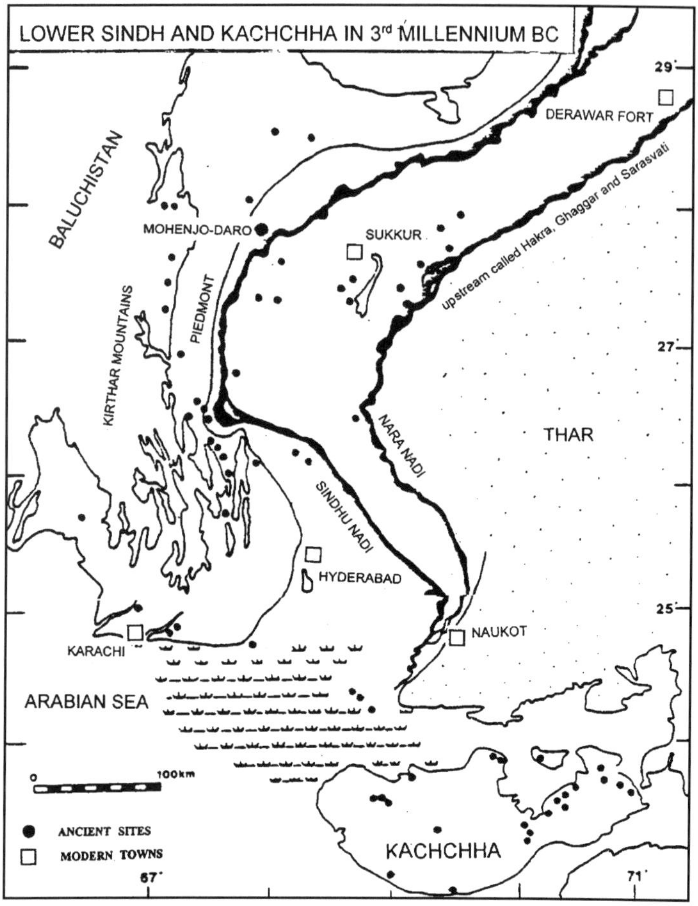

I. WERE THEN THE HARAPPANS THEMSELVES THE ṚIGVEDIC PEOPLE?

(I) INTRODUCTORY

The very raising of this question gives knee-jerks to certain scholars, since even at the dawn of the 21st century they remain wedded to the 19th century paradigms. Clinging tenaciously to those paradigms, they even today hold that: (i) the Vedas are no older than 1200 BCE; (ii) the Vedic people came from outside, as 'invaders' or, failing that, as 'immigrants'; and (iii) these people were nomads. In the previous Sections, we have given ample evidence to show

Fig. 4.14. Appearance of Bata-Markanda Divide.

that (i) the Vedas are decidedly much older that 1200 BCE and are to be placed at least in the third millennium BCE and (ii) the Vedic people were neither 'invaders' nor 'immigrants'. We now take up the third allegation, namely that the Vedic people were nomads, since this last allegation has become a great bugbear against an equation of the Harappans with the Vedic people.

(II) Were the Vedic People Nomads?

The Vedic people were no nomads wandering from place to place, but had regular settlements which were even fortified. This would be abundantly clear even from the few quotations that we give below from the *Ṛigveda* itself. For example, *RV* 7.15.14, runs as follows:

> *Adhā Mahī na āyasyanādhṛiṣṭo nṛipītaye pūrbhavā śatabhujiḥ*
>
> And, irresistible, be thou a mighty **metal fort to us,**
> **With hundred walls for man's defence**.

Through another verse, *RV* 10.101.8, the devotee prays that not only should the forts be metal-like strong, but that he should also be provided with many coats of armour, evidently signifying military strength:

.... varma sīvyadhvam bahulā pṛithūni
puraḥ kṛiṇudhvamāyasīradhṛiṣṭā

... stitch ye [oh gods] the **coats of armour**, wide and many; make **metal forts**, secure from all assailants.

On the economic front too, the Vedic people were quite affluent. They were engaged in both internal as well as overseas trade. This is clearly indicated by the following Ṛigvedic verse, 9.33.6:

rāyaḥ Samudrāññchaturo asmabhyam soma viśvataḥ. Ā pavasva sahasriṇaḥ

O Soma, from every side pour forth four seas filled with **a thousand-fold riches**.

In sea-trade, they used large-sized boats which were sometimes provided with a hundred (i.e. a large number of) oars. Says *RV* 1.116.5:

anārambhaṇe tadvīrayethāmanāsthāne agrabhaṇe samudre
yadaśvinā ūhathurbhujyumastam śatāritrām
nāvamātasthivānsam

O Asvins, you saved Bhujyu (from drowning) in a deep sea where there was nothing to hold on, by lifting him up in **a boat that had a hundred oars** and sending him to his place. This was indeed a brave act of yours.

Besides using bullock-carts, the Ṛigvedic people plied fast-running chariots, to which were sometimes yoked as many as four horses each, **bedecked with pearl ornaments.** This would be clear from the following (*RV* 1.126.4):

chatvārinśad daśarathasya śoṇāḥ sahasrasyāgre śreṇim nayanti
madachyutaḥ kṛiśanāvato atyān Kakṣīvanta udamṛikṣanta pajrāḥ

Forty bay horses of the ten cars' master before a thousand lead the long procession.
Feeling in joy Kakṣivān's sons and Pajrā's have grounded **the coursers decked with pearly trappings.**

In addition to the foregoing, the *Ṛigveda* throws valuable light on the social and political set-up of the times. This is self-evident from the occurrence in it of such terms as *sabhā* and *samiti* on the one hand and of *samrāṭ, rājan, rājaka,* etc. on the other. The first two terms clearly refer to assemblies that took vital decisions on matters of public interest. That there did exist these institutions in the Vedic society is clearly borne out by the following verse of the *Ṛigveda* (9.92.6):

pari sadmeva paśumānti hotā rajā na satyaḥ samitīriyānaḥ /
somaḥ punānaḥ kalaśāṁ ayāsīt sīdan mṛigo na mahiṣo vaneṣu //

As the priest seeks the station rich in cattle, **like a true king who goes to great assemblies,** Soma hath sought the pitchers while they cleansed him, and like a wild buffalo, in the wood hath settled.

In the above-noted verse, there are certain interesting similes, namely that the *Soma* enters the *kalaśa* (pitcher) just as the king enters the assembly or a wild buffalo enters the forests.

The other three terms, viz. *samrāṭ, rājan* and *rājaka*, point to a hierarchy of rulers. In *RV* 6.27.8, Abhyāvartī Chāyamāna is referred to as a Samrāṭ:

dvyāṁ Agne rathino viṁśatim gā vadhūmato maghavā mahyam samrāṭ /
Abhyāvartī Chāyamāno dadāti dūṇāśeyam dakṣiṇā pārthavānām //

Two wagon-teams, with damsels, twenty oxen, O Agni,
Abhyāvartin Chāyamāna,
The liberal Sovran, giveth me. This guerdon of Pṛithu's seed is hard to win from others.

In contrast, in *RV* 8.21.18 Chitra is said to be a *Rājan* while rulers of a lesser category were known as mere *Rājaka*s.

Chitra id rājā rājakā idanyake yake Sarasvatīmanu /
parjanya iva tatanaddhi vṛiṣṭyā sahasramayutā dadat //

Chitra is King, and only kinglings are the rest who dwell beside Sarasvatī.
He, like Parjanya with his rain, hath spread himself with thousand, yea, with myriad gifts.

Do such fine distinctions in matters of governance speak of a nomadic society? And let it be further stressed that these distinctions were very much real and not imaginary, as some diehards might think. This would be amply clear from the following quotation from the *Śatapatha Brāhmaṇa* (V.1.1.13):

> *Rājā vai Rājasūyeneṣṭvā bhavati, Samrād Vājapeyena / avaraṁ hi rājyaṁ*
> *paraṁ sāmrājyaṁ / Kāmayeta vai Rājā Samrāḍ bhavitum avaraṁ hi rājyam*
> *paraṁ samrājyaṁ / Na Samrāṭ kāmayeta Rājā bhavitum avaraṁ hi rājyaṁ paraṁ samrājyaṁ /*

> **By offering the *Rājasūya* he becomes Rājā and by the *Vājapeya* he becomes Samrāṭ, and the office of *Rājan* is lower and that of *Samraj* the higher. A Rājā might indeed wish to become a Samrāṭ, for the office of *Rājan* is lower and of *Samrāj* the higher; but the Samrāṭ would not wish to become a Rājā for the office of the *Rājan* is lower, and that of *Samrāj* the higher.**

I am afraid I have overburdened the reader with so many quotations from the *Ṛigveda* as also one from the *Śatapatha Brāhmaṇa*, but I thought it was well worth while doing so since I wanted the reader to feel a personal contact with these basic texts. Anyway, from the foregoing it must have become abundantly clear that the Ṛigvedic people were highly advanced on most fronts – social, economic and political. Do you think they have to be looked upon as 'nomads'?

(III) WAS THE HORSE UNKNOWN TO THE HARAPPANS?

But the ingrained apathy to a Harappan=Vedic equation does not end up there. There are two more objections which still remain to be addressed. First, it has been argued that during the Vedic times the horse was a well known animal, but the Harappan Civilization knew it not. Second, whereas the Vedic chariots were provided with spoked wheels, there were no spoked wheels during the Harappan times. If the opponents of the Harappan=Vedic equation adopt an ostrich-like attitude and do not look up to see the light thrown by recent excavations at a number of Harappan sites, whose fault is it? Anyway, for the sake of the reader, I briefly summarize the evidence on these two issues.

In respect of the absence of the horse from the Harappan Civilization a funny argument is often advanced, namely that this animal is not depicted on the Harappan seals whereas many other animals are. But why should we assume that the Harappans were out to produce a kind of zoo on their seals? The animals depicted thereon may have had some specific function to perform, such as being the insignia of the seal-owner and so on. That apart, why do these people not doubt the presence of the camel in the Harappan context, when this animal is also absent from the seals?

Anyway, let us move on to the positive evidence regarding the presence of the horse in the Harappan Civilization. In the report on his excavations at Mohenjo-daro, E.J.H. Mackay stated (1938, Vol. I, p. 289; Vol. II, pl. LXXVIII, no. 11): 'Perhaps the most interesting of the model animals is the one that **I personally take to represent a horse.**' Confirming this identification, Wheeler (1968: 92) observed: 'One terracotta, from a late level of Mohenjo-daro, seems to represent a horse, reminding us that a jaw-bone of a horse is also recorded from the same site, and that the horse was known at a considerably earlier period in Baluchistan.'

But much more evidence has come to light during the past five decades. For example, the Mature Harappan strata of Lothal in Gujarat, have yielded a terracotta figure of the horse (Fig. 3.15). And this is not the only evidence regarding the presence of the horse at Lothal. Reporting on the faunal remains from the site, two experts, namely Bholanath and G.V. Sreenivas Rao, state (in S.R. Rao 1985: 641): 'The single tooth of the horse referred to above indicates the presence of the horse at Lothal during the Harappan period. The tooth from Lothal resembles closely with that of the modern horse and has the pre-callabian (a minute fold near the base of the spur or protocone) which is a well distinguishable character of the cheek teeth of the horse.'

From Surkotada, another Harappan site in Gujarat, come a large number of bones of the horse (A.K. Sharma in Joshi 1990: 381). These were further examined by Professor Sandor Bokonyi, a renowned archaeozoologist and the then Director of the Archaeological Institute, Budapest, Hungary. And this is what he had to say:

> Through a thorough study of the equid remains of the protohistoric settlement of Surkotada Kutch, excavated under the direction of Dr. J.P. Joshi, I can state the following:

> The occurrence of true horse (*Equus Caballus* L.) was evidenced by the enamel pattern of the upper and lower cheek and teeth and by the size and form of the incisors and phalanges (toe bones). Since no wild horses lived in India in post-Pleistocene times, **the domestic nature of the Surkotada horse is undoubtful.** This is also supported by an inter-maxilla fragment whose incisor tooth shows clear signs of crib-biting, a bad habit only existing among domestic horses which are not extensively used for war.

Giving measurements, other details and photographs of the faunal remains in a paper published subsequently, Bokonyi (1997: 300) confirmed his findings: '**All in all, the evidence enumerated above undoubtedly raises the possibility of the occurrence of domesticated horses in the mature phase of the Harappa Culture, at the end of the third millennium BC.**'

However, those who have a mind-set to the contrary are not inclined to accept Bokonyi's well argued case. Thus, referring to a **discussion** that Meadow and Patel had with Bokonyi before the latter's death, they write (1997: 308): 'We went through each point that we had raised and in some cases agreed to disagree. **He (i.e. Bokonyi) remained firmly convinced that there are the bones of true horse *(Equus caballus)* in the Surkotada collection, and we remain skeptical.' While Meadow and Patel have every right to 'remain skeptical', it needs no emphasis that Bokonyi was an internationally acknowledged specialist on the anatomy of horses.**

Anyway, Rupnagar (formerly known as Ropar) in Panjab and Kalibangan in Rajasthan have also given evidence of the presence of the horse in Harappan context. At the latter site have been found an upper molar, a fragment of a shaft of distal end of femur and the distal end of left humerus (Sharma, A.K. 1993).

Though in the recent excavation at Harappa no horse bones have been met with, an earlier faunal collection from that site was examined by an expert of the Zoological Survey of India, Bholanath, who categorically stated that it did include the remains of the horse (Bholanath 1959).

From the foregoing it is clear that the Harappans did use the horse, although one would certainly welcome more and more evidence. As I have said elsewhere (Lal 1998: 109-12), the truant horse has cleared the hurdles!

(IV) WAS THE SPOKED WHEEL UNKNOWN TO THE HARAPPANS?

Equally untrue is the allegation that the Harappans did not know the spoked wheel. Although the hot and humid climate of our country does not permit the survival of wooden examples, terracotta models of the wheel clearly show that these were spoked. To substantiate this, we reproduce here one example each from the well known Harappan sites of Rakhigarhi and Banawali (Pls. XXXII and XXXIII respectively). In the former one sees clearly the painted spokes radiating from the central hub to the rim. The example from Banawali depicts the spokes in low relief. Perhaps it may not be out of place to add that this latter technique continued to be used even during the early historical times.

(V) THE CONCLUSION

In the foregoing paragraphs I have shown that all the objections raised against a Harappan=Vedic equation are baseless. Now, it is my turn to pose one and only one question to these learned scholars who swear that at no cost could the Harappans have been the Vedic people. This is contained in the following few lines.

Earlier I had shown that the *Ṛigveda* was decidedly earlier than 2000 BCE and may be placed anywhere in the 3rd millennium BCE. While discussing the identity of the Ṛigvedic Sarasvatī, I had also quoted Verses 5 and 6 of Hymn 75 of *Maṇḍala* 10 of the *Ṛigveda*. I am not repeating these here, but inquisitive readers may well go back to p. 115. To recall briefly, these verses show that the entire region from the upper Gaṅgā-Yamunā *doāb* on the east to the Indus and its western tributaries on the west was occupied by the Ṛigvedic people. The question that I now want to pose is: **'Archaeologically, which civilization was occupying this very area prior to 2000 BCE, namely during the period of the *Ṛigveda*?'** I would like to give these learned scholars some breathing time to ponder over the question. If they think

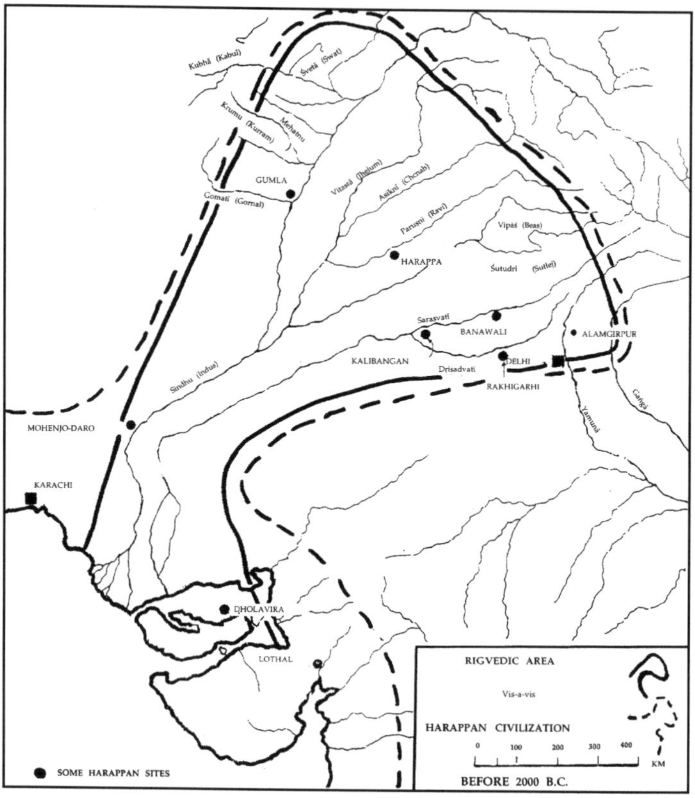

Fig. 4.15. Map showing a correlation between the Ṛigvedic area and the spread of the Harappan Civilization, before 2000 BCE.

coolly, shedding off all preconceived notions, I am sure their inescapable answer will be: '**The Harappan Civilization.**'

Hence the validity of the Harappan=Vedic equation (see Fig. 4.15).

CHAPTER FIVE

WERE THE HARAPPANS=VEDIC PEOPLE INDIGENOUS ?

As we have just seen, there is a very good case for the Harappans themselves having been the Vedic people, though no doubt one would like this equation to be further sealed by a satisfactory decipherment of the Harappan script. However, there remains one more issue which needs to be resolved. Were these people indigenous or did they come from outside?

With the discovery of the Harappan Civilization in the 1920s a natural question that began to be asked was whether this civilization grew up on the Indian soil itself or it was an import from elsewhere. It was suggested by certain scholars that West Asia, where civilizations going back to the 4th-3rd millennia BCE had already been discovered, must have been at the root of this newly discovered Indian civilization. However, when the protagonists of the West-Asian origin were called upon to point out which constituents of the Harappan Civilization were identical with those of the West-Asian civilization concerned, they fumbled, as there was indeed nothing to support their thesis. They then took recourse to a strange theory, viz. 'ideas have wings', suggesting that, if not the actual civilization itself, the 'idea' of civilization must have travelled from West Asia. What a proposition!

The foregoing baseless theory has since been given up because **excavations carried out during the past fifty years**

have revealed a fool-proof story of the gradual evolution of the Harappan Civilization on the soil of the Indo-Pakistan subcontinent itself. Among the more important sites which have yielded evidence of settlements well antedating the Mature Harappan stage mention may be made of: Mehrgarh, Kot Diji, Harappa itself, Gumla, Rehman Dheri, etc. in Pakistan; and Kalibangan, Banawali, Rakhigarhi, Kunal and Bhirrana in the Sarasvatī Valley in India. (Cf. Lal 1997: 32-91. Bhirrana was not included in this book, since it had not been excavated by that time.) There are at least two stages that preceded the Mature Harappan. The immediately preceding one is known variously as Kot Diji/Sothi/ Kalibangan I Culture. It is assignable to a period from the last quarter of the fourth to the first quarter of third millennium BCE. There is yet another earlier stage, known as Hakra/Ravi Culture, going back to the beginning of the fourth millennium BCE or even somewhat earlier. This last-named stage is now being also revealed in the Sarasvatī Valley. At Bhirrana in Haryana, the relevant Carbon-14 dates associated with this stage are as follows (L.S. Rao 2005: 67):

> Sample No. BS 2314. Calibrated age: 1 Sigma 4770 (4536, 4506, 4504) 4353 BCE
> Sample No. BS 2318. Calibrated age: 1 Sigma 5336 (5041) 4721 BCE
> Sample No. BS 2333. Calibrated age: 1 Sigma 6647 (6439) 6221 BCE

Even if we temporarily ignore Sample No. BS 2333, the other two samples clearly show that the ancestry of the Harappan Civilization in the Sarasvatī Valley goes back to the beginning of the fifth millennium BCE. For all one knows, there may turn up one day even a still earlier stage.

It would thus be seen that **the Harappans were deeply rooted in the Indian soil. Therefore, the Vedic people, being identical with the Harappans as shown earlier, were indigenous.**

CHAPTER SIX

DID SOME VEDIC PEOPLE EMIGRATE WESTWARDS, OUT OF INDIA ?

The answer to the above-mentioned question is an unhesitating 'Yes'. It comes from three, completely independent, areas, two of which are separated from each other by thousands of kilometres, while the third one lies in between them. These areas are: (i) Turkey in the west; (ii) India in the east; and (iii) Iran in the middle.

Turkey has yielded incontrovertible inscriptional evidence about the presence of the Aryans in that region at least as far back as the 14th century BCE. The entire community of historians and archaeologists was struck with surprise when in the first decade of the 20th century Hugo Winckler discovered in his excavations at Bogazkoy certain inscribed clay tablets on which was recorded a treaty between a Mitanni king named Matiwaza and a Hittite king, Suppiluliuma, ascribable to circa 1380 BCE. As witnesses to this treaty the two rulers invoked the following Vedic gods: *Indara* (=Vedic *Indra*), *Mitras (il)* (=Vedic *Mitra*), *Nasatia*(*nna*) (=Vedic *Nāsatya*) and *Uruvanass(il)* (=Vedic *Varuṇa*).

And the treaty is only a chip of the large block. From this region and its neighbourhood more than a hundred names have come to light which have a Sanskrit stamp on them: such as: *Biridasva* (=Vedic *Vṛidhāśva*); *Urudīti*, a Hurrian king (=Skt. *Urudīti*); *Artasumara*, another Mitanni king (=Vedic

Ṛitasmara, in addition to *Matiwaza* = *Mativāja*, already mentioned), and so on. The context of some of these names goes back to the seventeenth century BCE. Then there is another remarkable document. It deals with the technique of horse-training and mentions Sanskrit numerals like *ekavartana, trivartana*, etc. meaning thereby that the horse under training should be made to make one round, three rounds and so on of the race-course.

Though the foregoing data are enough to establish the presence of Vedic Aryans in ancient Turkey, there is yet another kind of evidence to which attention may be drawn. In the Mitannian art, dating at least to the 16th-17th century BCE (perhaps even to circa 2100 BCE), there is the portrayal of the peacock – a bird typical of India. This couldn't have been the case unless Indians were behind the inspiration.

Commenting on the Bogazkoy evidence, the renowned Indologist T. Burrow observed (1955): 'The Ayrans appear in Mitanni from 1500 BC as the ruling dynasty, which means that **they must have entered the country as conquerors**.' 'Conquerors from where', may not one ask? At that point of time **there was no other country in the entire world *except India* where the above-mentioned gods were worshipped. And since, as has already been shown earlier, the *Ṛigveda decidedly belonged to a period prior to 2000 BCE*, there is no chronological obstacle in such a hypothesis.**

In this context, let the reader be told that this very Bogazkoy evidence was given a different twist by certain scholars in the past. While admitting that the gods mentioned in the treaty were Indo-Aryan, they argued that these people were on their way to India. They took this stand because in those days, as per Max Muller's fatwa, the Vedas were considered to have been only as old as 1200 BCE whereas the Bogazkoy inscription was dated to the 14th century BCE. Now that we know full well that the Vedas are in no case posterior to 2000 BCE, that kind of argument is no longer valid.

Again, some scholars have even gone to the extent of saying that this very region was the 'original home' of the Aryans. But this stand, again, is fundamentally incorrect. Why? Because when we say that such and such area was the 'original home' of a people called X, we mean that the local population was by and large that of X and was **rooted** in the area. But this was not the case with the Bogazkoy region.

The local population was different and the Aryans were only the rulers, coming from outside, as shown by Burrow. Had they constituted the core or base of the population, they and their language would have 'lived on and on', which is not the case.

The evidence from Iran is no less revealing. The sacred book of the Zoroastrians, viz. the *Āvestā*, is language-wise very close to but later than the *Ṛigveda.* A conspicuous difference is that the Ṛigvedic 's' becomes 'h' in the *Āvestā.* Content-wise, the Āvestan religion reflects a kind of dissent from that of the *Ṛigveda.* The concepts of *Deva*s and *Asura*s get reversed. Nevertheless, there is a genetic relationship between the two. All this shows that the Āvestan people are closely related but posterior to the Ṛigvedic people – a situation which can only be explained by some of the Ṛigvedic people having moved to the land of the *Āvestā.* There are many pieces of internal evidence in the *Āvestā* itself which testify to this. For example, the *Āvestā* refers to *Yoi hapta Hendu* which is none else than the *Sapta Sindhu* of the *Ṛigveda.* Such a mention of the Ṛigvedic land of 'Seven Rivers' (*Sapta Sindhu*) in the *Āvestā* can only mean that the Āvestan people continued to cherish the memory of that Ṛigvedic land – a clear indication of the westward movement of the Ṛigvedic people.

However, it is not unlikely that the section of the Ṛigvedic people that finally settled down in Persia, may have, on the way, sojourned for some time in Afghanistan, during which period the aforesaid linguistic and religious changes would have taken place.

It may not be out of place to have a word about the make-up, region of the composition and the date of the *Āvestā.* The *Āvestā* has two major divisions, generally referred to as 'Old' and 'Young'. The 'Old' comprises *Gāthā*s which are believed to have been composed by Zarathustra himself. It also has a part known as *Yasna Haptanghaiti* of which the authorship is not known. The 'Young' *Āvestā* comprises many an item such as religio-legal texts, hymns devoted to certain deities, etc. All available evidence suggests that the *Āvestā* was composed most probably in northeastern Iran. As regards the date, the issue is somewhat controversial. According to one view, it may well go back to circa 14th-11th century BCE, while another view would bring it down to 8th-7th century BCE.

While the debate about the exact date of the *Āvestā* would continue until some clinching evidence becomes available, it may interest the reader that the region mentioned as **Parśvaḥ** in a Vedic text, *Baudhāyana Śrautasūtra* (to be discussed next), is also mentioned by almost the same name in a completely independent document thousands of kilometres west of India. Dated to 835 BCE, it states that king Shalmaneser of Assyria received tributes from **27** kings of **Parsuwas**. That would imply that by the ninth century BCE, the **Pārśvas** had fully established themselves in the region and had evidently reached there several centuries before – maybe by the middle of the second millennium BCE. All this would give legitimacy to the above-mentioned early date both for the *Āvestā* as well as for the migration of the **Pārśvas** from India to Iran some time in the second millennium BCE.

Finally, to come to the evidence from India itself, endorsing an emigration of the Vedic Aryans out of India, to three contiguous regions towards the west. A Vedic text, namely the *Baudhāyana Śrautasūtra* (18.44), runs as follows (cf. Fig. 6.1 for the original):

> *Prāṇāyauḥ pravavrāja tasyaite Kurū-Pañchālāḥ Kāśī-Videhā ity etad*
> *Āyavam pravrājam Pratyaṅ Amāvasus tasyaite* ***Gāndhārayas Parśvo Arāṭṭā*** *itya etad Āmāvasavam*

Translated into English, the Sanskrit text avers:

Āyu migrated eastwards. His (progeny) are the Kurū-Pāñchālas and Kāśi-Videhas. This is Āyava migration. Amāvasu migrated westwards. **His (progeny) are the Gāndhārī, Paraśu and Āraṭṭa. This is the Amāvasva migration.**

The details of these migrations are as follows. Aila Pururavas and Urvaśī had two sons, named Āyu and Amāvasu. They migrated, respectively to the east and west. The former, moving eastwards, gave rise to the Kurū-Pāñchāla and Kāśi-Videha dynasties, while the latter, moving out to the west, went over to Gāndhāra, Parśu and Araṭṭa. This bifurcation evidently took place in an area which was between the Kurū region on the east and the Gāndhāra region on the west. In other words, the scene of partition lay somewhere in Panjab.

[१८ । ४४, ४५ ।]   बौधायनश्रौतसूत्रम् ।   ३९७

अथ यद्रहरागच्छेयुस्तदानग्ना स्यां । न त्वा नग्नं पश्येयमिति । सर्वमेवैतद्भगवति सुकरमिति होवाच । कथा त्वपि[1] जाया पतिं नग्नं न पश्यतीत्यन्तर्वासं वसीथा[2] इति होवाचानग्नो भवेति[3] । तथा सहोवाचान्तर्वासं वसानः । सा ह स्म जाताञ्जातानेव पुत्रानपविध्यति । ताँ ह राजोवाच पुत्रकामा ह वै भगवति वयं मनुष्याः स्मो जाताञ्जातांस्तु त्वमपविध्यसीति । सा होवाच पर्यवेतरात्रयो भवन्ति क्षीणायुषो ऽन्ये । भूयः प्रियं करवावहा इति । आयुं[4] चामावसुं च जनयां चकार । सा होवाचेमौ बिभृतेमौ[5] सर्वमायुरेष्यत इति । प्राङायुः प्रवव्राज । तस्यैते कुरुपञ्चालाः[6] काशिविदेहा इत्येतदायवं प्रव्राजं । प्रत्यङमावसुस्तस्यैते गान्धारय[7] स्पर्शवो ऽराट्टा इत्येतदामावसवम्[8] । ॥ ४४ ॥

अथो हास्या एषा पूर्वचित्तिरप्सरा स्वसा बभूव । सा हेर्ष्यां चक्रे ज्योग् वै मे स्वसा मनुष्येष्ववात्सीद्धन्तैनामच्छाया-

१ त्वपि L, त्वयि the other MSS.

२ वसीथा L Be (sec. m.) वासीत्यास्य the other MSS.

३ भवति MSS. exc. L, which has वेम ह वासनो भवतीति ।

४ प्रायुं Be (sec. m.).

५ बिभृते॰ Be L ; the other MSS. om. these words.

६ ॰पांचालाः L B.

७ The proper names given acc. to Be (sec. m.) ; the other MSS. गांधारा (or री) पयस्पर्शवोद्दारा (or त्य) मा (or वा) ।

८ इत्येतच्चावसुम् or इत्येतन्मामवसुम् or इत्येतन्मामावसम् MSS.

Fig. 6.1. Photocopy of the relevant Sanskrit text from the *Baudhāyana Śrautasūtra.*

The identification of the destinations arrived at by the two branches poses no problem. The Kurū-Pāñchāla territory lay in eastern Haryana and western Uttar Pradesh. The Kāśi-Videhas were settled in eastern Uttar Pradesh and western Bihar. Of the territories reached by the western branch, Gāndhāra is straightaway identifiable. It is the Kandahar

MIGRATION OF PEOPLE AS MENTIONED IN THE *BAUDHĀYANA ŚRAUTASŪTRA*

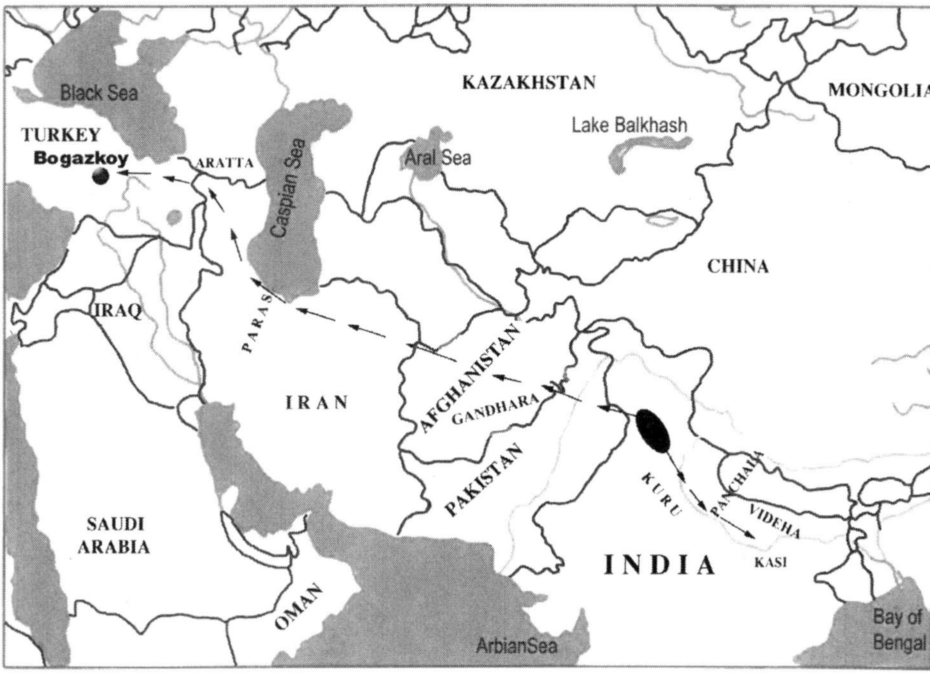

Fig. 6.2. Migration of People as mentioned in the *Baudhāyana Śrautasūtra*.

province of Afghanistan. Likewise, Parśu is identifiable with Persia, which was renamed 'Iran' only as recently as 1935. It is only the location of Araṭṭa that has caused some debate.

This place (Araṭṭa) is mentioned not only in the above-referred-to Vedic text but also in an epic thousands of kilometres away in the west, in Iraq. The epic, ascribable to the end of the 3rd millennium BCE, mentions that Enmerkar, king of Uruk, sent a messenger, making certain demands, to Ensuhgiranna, the ruler of Araṭṭa. We are not concerned here with the other details of the story, but only with the identification of Araṭṭa. Some scholars identify it with Ziroft, while some others with Ararat. Fed up with the unending debate, some even go to extent of calling it unreal and a mere 'concoction' by the composer of the epic. Our failure to arrive at a consensus regarding the identification of the place is no justification for calling it a 'concoction'. You can't throw the baby away with the bath-tub. Black, Cunningham, et al. (in an Internet presentation) place Araṭṭa in 'the snow-capped mountains that border Mesopotamia'. Further, in a section of the poem, the ruler of Araṭṭa tells the messenger: '... The queen of heaven and earth, the goddess of the numerous *me*, holy Inana, **has brought to Araṭṭa, the mountain of shining** ***me, I whom she has let bar the entrance of the mountains as if with a great door. ..***'. From the foregoing account it would appear that Araṭṭa was located close to an opening (pass) in the mountains which the ruler of Araṭṭa could easily seal. All this enhances the claim of the Ararat region, located close on the north of Iraq, in a mountainous terrain, as being Araṭṭa of the Sumerian epic. Further, if on grounds of phonetic similarity Gāndhāra and Parśu of the Vedic text can be identified respectively with Kandahar and Persia, and Susin and Ansan, mentioned in the Sumerian epic, with Susa and Ansan, what, may one ask, is the reason to discard that very principle in the case Araṭṭa? It, therefore, stands to reason that the proposed identification by some scholars of Araṭṭa with Ararat in the Armenian region, to the northwest of Persia, may be in order. In that case, the Vedic Aryans, emigrating out of India travelled via Kandahar and Persia (Iran) to Ararat, following a south-of-the-Caspian-Sea route. And since from Ararat to Turkey is just a next-door affair, the immigration of the Vedic Aryans into Turkey becomes self-explained. Further, as there are enough dated records on the Turkey side, the emigration from India is easily assignable to the first half of the second millennium BCE. (Cf. Fig. 6.2.)

CHAPTER SEVEN

The Emergent Picture

Looking back, one finds that the most ancient civilization of India, known variously as the Harappan, Indus or Indus-Sarasvatī Civilization, was indeed remarkable in may respects. It may not have given to the world the high-rising pyramids of Giza or the immensely rich royal tombs of Ur, but it has shown how an ideal and well balanced community lives – in which the differences between the rich and the poor are not glaring. In the other two countries, symbolized respectively by the pyramids and the royal tombs, the haves had it all, while the have-nots none at all.

Though certain areas in the Harappan settlements have been designated as 'citadels', these did not contain any 'palaces', but mainly religious structures and residences of the priestly class and perhaps of the elites. The agricultural and trading communities too were well provided for. And although there was a class of workmen, they were not required to drag massive stones up to the top of the pyramids, completely exhausted and famished at the end. In the Harappan set-up, they were making ceramics, thrashing grains, working in metal furnaces, and so on. But the society did recognize their needs and provided them with well-planned residential complexes (such as at Harappa), though on a moderate scale. In essence, the Harappan societal scenario was not that of 'exploitation', but of mutual 'accommodation'.

As in life so in death, the situation was no different. There are no 'royal graves' at any of the Harappan sites. There were no forced interments of the servants along with their masters as in Mesopotamia. All the discovered graves are more or less on the same pattern – a sign of egalitarianism.

The Harappans showed to the world what an ideal town-planning could be. Enclosed by a peripheral wall, the township had a series of streets, running north-south and east-west. At many of the settlements there was a well laid-out, underground drainage system. To the Harappans also goes the credit of using kiln-fired bricks. Among other things, the superbly carved steatite seals and the lovely little dancing damsel cannot but make anyone hold his breath.

Though in its Mature stage the Harappan Civilization is datable from 2600-2000 BCE, there is enough evidence to show that its earlier stages go back to the fifth millennium BCE. Further field-work might bring to light even deeper roots.

In the report on his excavations at Harappa, Sir Mortimer Wheeler passed two very bold judgements. One, that there was an 'Aryan Invasion' of India which destroyed the Harappan Civilization, and the other that as a result of this invasion the Harappan Civilization became 'extinct'. However, as subsequent researches have clearly proved, neither of these assertions is correct. There is no evidence of an invasion at any of the hundreds of Harappan sites, much less by the Aryans.

Nor is there any evidence of the extinction of the Harappan Culture. Due to a variety of reasons the urban scenario did no doubt gradually decline, but the people and their culture continued to thrive. In Chapter II we have shown how in almost every walk of life even today the traits of the Harappan Culture are met with – whether it is agriculture, or yoga or religious beliefs and practices or even the make-up by ladies. The spirit of India lives on!

Once it became clear to the 'invasionists' that there was no chance to hold on to the 'Invasion' thesis, they took recourse to another route, viz. that of 'Immigration'. They averred that then the Vedic Aryans must have 'immigrated' from the Bactria-Margiana Archaeological Complex (BMAC) of Central Asia. This thesis too has been examined in depth in Chapter IV and it turns out that there is no evidence to sustain it either. Most importantly, not even a single characteristic feature of the BMAC ever appeared east of the Indus – the main domain of the Vedic people. Thus, both the theories, viz. those of 'Invasion' and 'Immigration', fall to the ground.

Completely road-blocking these theories are also the sciences of human biology and human genetics. A careful study of the human skeletal remains has proved that there was no entry of a new set of people into India between 4500 BCE and 800 BCE. Likewise, Y-chromosomal data also argue against an influx of people from regions north and north-west of India. In fact, these data point to 'the diffusion of some Indian-specific lineages northward'.

All these theories apart, the basic question is: Who were after all the authors of this great civilization of India? An initial fatwa given by the German scholar Max Muller in the 19th century that the Vedas were only as old as 1200 BCE stands at the root of the entire confusion. Thus, when the Harappan Civilization was discovered in the 1920s and dated to the 3rd millennium BCE (on the basis of the occurrence of many Harappan objects in the already-dated strata of the Mesopotamian culture), it was argued that since the Vedas were only as old as 1200 BCE, the Harappan Culture could not have been of the Vedic people. And since the only other major linguistic group in the country is the Dravidian one, it was easily assumed that the authors of the Harappan Civilization spoke a Dravidian tongue. As detailed in Chapter IV, there are many fallacies in this thesis, which need not be gone into all over once again. In fact, barring a few entrenched ones, no scholar stands by the Harappan=Dravidian thesis.

Now, if the Harappans were not Dravidian-speakers, were they the Sanskrit-speaking Vedic people? Against this equation four objections have been raised from time to time, namely that (i) the Vedic people were nomads whereas the Harappans were urbanized; (ii) the Vedic people used the horse, while the Harappans did not; (iii) the Vedas refer to the spoked wheel, but the Harappan people did not know it; and (iv) according to Max Muller's dating, the Vedas were only as old as 1200 BCE, whereas the Harappan Civilization belonged to the 3rd millennium BCE. All these objections have been examined thoroughly in Chapter IV and have been found to be baseless.

Further, the combined evidence of archaeology, hydrology, geology and radiocarbon-dating has established that the Sarasvatī, which has been referred to a number of times in the *Ṛigveda* as a mighty flowing river, dried up around 2000 BCE. In other words, **the *Ṛigveda* is older than 2000 BCE**. (How much older, it is anybody's guess.) The *Ṛigveda* also spells out the area occupied by the Vedic people: it extended from the Indus on the west to the upper reaches of the Yamunā-Gaṅgā on the east. And if a simple question is now posed, viz. archaeologically, **which civilization flourished in this very area prior to 2000 BCE, the inescapable answer will have to be: 'The Harappan Civilization'. It is thus abundantly clear that the authors of the Harappan Civilization were none else than the Vedic people themselves (Fig. 4.15).**

Finally, a no less interesting aspect of the issue. Some time in the second millennium BCE the Vedic Indians themselves ventured to emigrate westwards. This is vouchsafed by many a document unearthed in ancient Turkey, particularly by the well known treaty between a Mitanni king named Matiwaza and a Hittite king Suppiluliuma, dated to the 14th century BCE. They invoke as witnesses the Vedic gods Indra, Mitra, Nāsatyas and Varuṇa. What more evidence is needed to prove the Vedic presence there?

The most ancient religious text of the Parsis, viz. the *Āvestā*, also affirms this emigration. On linguistic grounds the *Āvestā* is a younger sister of the Vedas, but it portrays a picture of some kind of religious dissent from the elder. In it is also mentioned the land of *Hapta Hendu*, which is none other than the *Sapta Sindhu* of the *Ṛigveda*. (It is well known that the '*s*' of Vedic Sanskrit changes to '*h*' of the Avestan language.) All this cannot be brushed under the carpet.

Last but not the least comes the affirmative statement by a Vedic text itself, namely the *Baudhāyana Śrautasūtra*, which clearly refers to the emigration of a section of the Vedic people westwards – to Gāndhāra (modern Kandhar Province of Afghanistan), Parśu (Persia) and further west to Araṭṭa (modern Ararat), bordering on Turkey where the aforementioned inscription mentioning Vedic deities has been found (Fig. 6.2).

Isn't all this thought-provoking?

Bibliography

Bholanath. 1959. Remains of the horse and Indian elephant from the protohistoric site of Harappa (West Pakistan). *Proceeding of First All India Congress of Zoologists*, pt. 2, pp. 1-14.

Bisht, R.S. 1991. Dholavira: New Horizons of the Indus Civilization. *Purātattva*, 20: 71-82.

——. 1994. Banawali. In J.P. Joshi and R.S. Bisht. *India and the Indus Civilization*, pp. 23-31. New Delhi.

Bokonyi, S. 1997. Horse Remains from the Prehistoric Site of Surkotada, Kutch, Late Third Millennium BC. *South Asian Archaeology*, 13: 297-307.

Burrow, T. 1955 (reprint). *The Sanskrit Language*. Faber and Faber.

Dales, G.F. 1964. The Mythical Massacre at Mohenjo-daro. *Expedition*, 6(3):36-43.

Danino, M. 2006. *L'Inde et l'invasion de nulle part*. Paris: Le Belles Lettres.

Dhavalikar, M.K. and Shubhangana Atre. 1989. The Fire Cult and Virgin Sacrifice: Some Harappan Rituals. In J.M. Kenoyer (ed.), *Old Problems and New Perspectives in the Archaeology of South Asia*, Wisconsin Archaeological Reports, Vol. 2, pp.193-205.

Griffith, R.T.H. 1995 (reprint). *The Hymns of the Ṛigveda*. Delhi: Low Price Publications.

Gupta, S.P. (under print). Did the BMAC ever cross the Indus? Paper presented at an international conference held at Vadodara in 2005.

Habib, Irfan and Faiz Habib. 1991-92. The Historical Geography of India, 1800-800 BC. *Proceedings Indian History Congress: 52nd Session*, pp. 72-97.

Hemphill, B.E. et al. 1991. Biological Adaptations and Affinities of Bronze Age Harappans. In R.H. Meadow (ed.), *Harappa Excavations 1986-1990*, pp. 137-82. Madison, Wisconsin: Prehistory Press.

Joshi, J.P. 1990. *Excavation at Surkotada 1971-72 and Exploration in Kutch.* New Delhi: Archaeological Survey of India.

Kazanas, N.D. 2001. A New Date for the *Ṛgveda. Journal of Indian Council of Philosophical Research,* Special Issue, pp. 79-108.

Kenoyer, J.M. 1998. *Ancient Cities of the Indus Civilization.* Karachi: Oxford University Press and American Institute of Pakistan Studies.

Lal, B.B. 1966. The Direction of Writing in the Harappan Script. *Antiquity*, XL(157): 52-55.

——. 1997. *The Earliest Civilization of South Asia.* New Delhi: Aryan Books International.

——. 1998. *India 1947-1997: New Light on the Indus Civilization.* New Delhi: Aryan Books International.

——. 2002. *The Sarasvati Flows On: The Continuity of Indian Culture.* New Delhi: Aryan Books International.

——. 2005. *The Homeland of the Aryans: Evidence of Rigvedic Flora and Fauna & Archaeology.* New Delhi: Aryan Books International.

——. 2007. Let Not the 19th Century Paradigms Continue to Haunt Us. *Purātattva*, No. 37 (2006-07), pp. 1-19.

Ligabue, G. and S. Salvatori. 1989. *Bactria: an Ancient Civilization from the Sands of Afghanistan.* Venezia.

Mackay, E.J.H. 1938. *Further Excavations at Mohenjo-daro.* 2 vols. Delhi: Government of India.

——. 1943 (reprint 1976). *Chanhu-daro Excavations 1935-36.* Delhi: Bhartiya Publishing House.

Marshall, John. 1931. *Mohenjo-daro and the Indus Civilization.* 3 vols. London: Arthur Probsthain.

Meadow, R. and A. Patel. 1997. A Comment on 'Horse Remains from Surkotada' by Sandor Bokonyi. *South Asian Archaeology*, 13: 308-15.

Muller, F. Max. 1890 (reprint 1979). *Physical Religion.* New Delhi: Asian Educational Services.

Nath, Amarendra. 1998-99. Further Excavations at Rakhigarhi. *Purātattva*, 29: 46-49.

Nyberg, Harri. 1995. The Problem of the Aryans and the Soma: The Botanical Evidence. In G. Erdosy (ed.), *The Indo-Aryans of Ancient South Asia,* pp. 382-406. Berlin: Walter de Gruyter.

Possehl, Gregory L. 1996. *The Indus Age: The Writing System.* New Delhi: Oxford and IBH Publishing Co. Pvt. Ltd.

Possehl, Gregory L. et al. 2004. The Ahar-Banas Complex and the BMAC. *Man and Environment,* Vol. XXIX, No. 2, pp. 18-29.

Puri, V.M.K. and B.C. Verma. 1998. Glaciological and Geological Source of Vedic Saraswati in the Himalayas. *Itihas Darpan*, Vol. IV, No. 2: 7-36.

Raikes, Robert. 1968. Kalibangan: Death from Natural Causes. *Antiquity*, XLII: 286-91.

Rao, L.S. 2005. New Light on the Excavation of Harappan Settlement at Bhirrana. *Purātattva*, No. 35 (2004-2005), pp. 60-68.

Rao, S.R. 1979. *Lothal – A Harappan Port Town (1955-62)*, Vol. I. New Delhi: Archaeological Survey of India.

——. 1985. *Lothal – A Harappan Port Town (1955-62)*,Vol. II. New Delhi: Archaeological Survey of India.

Renfrew, C. 1988. *Archaeology and Language*. New York: Cambridge University Press.

Sahoo, Sanghamitra, et al. 2006. A Prehistory of Indian Y Chromosomes: Evaluating Demic Diffusion Scenarios. *PNAS*, Vol. 103, No. 4: 843-48.

Sarianidi, V.I. 1993 a. Margiana and the Indo-Iranian World. *South Asian Archaeology*, Vol. II, pp. 667-80.

——. 1993 b. Margiana in the Ancient Orient. In IASCCA *Information Bulletin*, 19, pp. 5-28. Nauka.

——. 2002. *Margush: Ancient Oriental Kingdom in the Old Delta of the Murghab River*. Ashgabat.

Shaffer, Jim.G. and Diane Lichtenstein. 1999. Migration, Philology and South Asian Archaeology. In Johannes Bronkhorst and Madhav M. Deshpande (eds.), *Aryan and Non-Aryan in South Asia: Evidence, Interpretation and Ideology*. Cambridge: Harvard University.

Shah, Sayid Ghulam Mustafa and Asko Parpola (eds.). 1991. *Corpus of Indus Seals and Inscriptions: 2. Collection in Pakistan*. Helsinki: Suomalainen Tiedeakatemia.

Sharma, A.K. 1993. The Harappan Horse was buried under Dune of ..... *Purātattva*, 23:30-34.

Sharma, R.S. 1999. *Advent of the Aryans in India*. New Delhi: Manohar Publishers.

Thapar, Romila. 1988-91. In *Journal Asiatic Society of Bombay*, Vol. 64-66, pp. 259-60.

Vats, M.S. 1940 (reprint 1974). *Excavations at Harappa*. Delhi: Bhartiya Publishing House.

Valdia, K.S. 2002. *Sarasvati: The River that Disappeared*. Hyderabad: Universities Press (India) Limited.

Wheeler, R.E.M. 1947. Harappa 1946: The Defences and Cemetery R 37. *Ancient India*, 3:58-130.

——. 1968. *The Indus Civilization*. 3rd edn. Cambridge: University Press.

Witzel, M. 1995. Ṛigvedic History: poets, chieftains and polities. In George Erdosy (ed.), *The Indo-Aryans of Ancient South Asia*, pp. 307-52. Berlin: Walter de Gruyter.

Index

THE BOOK

Since 1997 Professor Lal has published several books dealing with various aspects of the archaeology of ancient India and the Vedic literature. But all these were research-oriented. He thus felt that there was a need to address the common reader. Hence the present book.

Professor Lal tells the reader, with ample photographic illustrations, that almost every aspect of Indian culture is deeply rooted in the past, which is at least 5,000 years old. He then gives an integrated picture of the civilization of those days —variously called the Harappan, Indus or Indus-Sarasvatī Civilization. Thereafter he deals with the ethnicity of the authors of this great civilization. With solid arguments, he refutes the theories that there was an 'Aryan Invasion' of India, which destroyed the Harappan Civilization or that there was an immigration of the (BMAC) people from Central Asia. He demonstrates that in all likelihood the Harappans themselves were the Vedic people and were indigenous. Further, archaeological and literary evidences combine to suggest that some time in the second millennium BCE a section of the Vedic people themselves emigrated westwards to Iran and even up to Turkey, contributing their mite to the local culture.

It is hoped that the reader will enjoy going through this book.

THE AUTHOR

A world-renowned archaeologist, **Prof. B.B. Lal** was the Director General of the Archaeological Survey of India from 1968 to 1972. In the latter year he took voluntary retirement to pursue his research programmes independently. First he joined Jiwaji University, Gwalior, as a Professor and later the Indian Institute of Advanced Study, Shimla, of which he was also the Director.

Professor Lal's excavations cover a very wide range — from palaeolithic times to early historical. At Kalibangan, Rajasthan, he unearthed a prosperous city of the Harappan Civilization. The excavations at Hastināpura, Indraprastha, etc. have established that there was a kernel of truth in the *Mahābhārata*, even though the epic is full of interpolations. Likewise, his excavations at Ayodhyā, Śṛiṅgaverapura, etc. have indicated that the *Rāmāyaṇa* too has a basis in history.

In recognition of his contribution to archaeology, the President of India honoured him in 2000 with the award of ***Padma Bhūṣaṇa***.